BEAUTIFUL
COOKIES FOR ALL

THE EASY WAY TO DECORATE STUNNING DESIGNS WITH BUTTERCREAM

MELISSA BROYLES

CREATOR OF SUGARBOMBE

PAGE STREET
PUBLISHING CO.

PAGE STREET
PUBLISHING CO.

First published in 2023 by
Page Street Publishing Co.
27 Congress Street, Suite 1511
Salem, MA 01970
www.pagestreetpublishing.com

Distributed by Macmillan, sales in Canada by The Canadian Manda Group.

27   26   25   24   23   1   2   3   4   5

ISBN-13: 978-1-64567-735-2
ISBN-10: 1-64567-735-4

Library of Congress Control Number: 2022915703

Cover and book design by Laura Benton for Page Street Publishing Co.
Photography by Melissa Broyles

Printed and bound in the China

CONTENTS

INTRODUCTION

I have always believed in the power of cookies. Through my culinary journey, I have learned how food, especially of the sweeter variety, has the power to create a little bit of magic.

I grew up in rural North Dakota where baking was part of everyday life. From those early days with an Easy-Bake Oven watching chocolate cakes rise under the heat of a 100-watt lightbulb, to baking elaborate cakes for weddings, cookies have been there, not always front and center, but always waiting in the wings for their moment. Creating my company Sugarbombe and writing this book helped to usher in that moment and allowed me to fully explore the world of cookies.

In my mind, those are the important moments: the moments you spend with family baking on cold winter days, the moments when you are grieving a loss, the moments when you are celebrating a birth. Cookies are a simple gift you give a new neighbor to welcome them to the neighborhood. They are stuffed with ice cream and eaten with laughter by the pool on hot summer days. They are a sweet little treat you sneak into a lunch box. They are part of life and every celebration, big or small.

Beautiful Cookies for All was created in the hope that everyone will feel empowered to create culinary magic for those closest to their hearts, to celebrate anything and everything. To inspire a day of baking and creating with friends and family. To spend time creating for those in your community.

COOKIE BASICS

ROLLING OUT THE DOUGH

When using stencils and hand-cutting shapes, chill the dough so you will get a clean edge. Letting the dough rest in the refrigerator does two things: It firms up the fat, making the dough easier to handle, and it also relaxes the gluten, leading to more tender cookies.

Chill the dough for at least 30 minutes, or up to 1 week. After chilling the dough, let it rest at room temperature for at least 30 minutes. When you work with it, the dough should be cool but not cold to the touch.

Before rolling, form the dough into a rectangular shape. Give the dough a light dusting of flour to prevent the rolling pin from sticking. You can roll the dough on a piece of parchment paper or a self-healing mat (see page 11). If you are using parchment paper, you may need to sprinkle a little flour on the parchment to keep the dough from sticking. If using a self-healing mat, you will not need to use flour on the mat. Keep in mind that the dough becomes tougher the more you roll and reroll. The more flour you add will also make the cookies drier and tougher. Work efficiently and with the least amount of flour possible.

Working on the parchment paper or self-healing mat, start in the center of the dough and roll outward. Work your way around the dough toward the edge of the parchment paper or self-healing mat with outward, even strokes. The dough should be as level as possible. If the cookies are uneven, they may bake unevenly. There are a few items that can help with this. Silicone guide bands or rings (see page 10) are one helpful solution. Repeat the rolling process with any remaining disks of dough.

Place all sheets of dough on a half sheet pan lined with parchment paper. Stack the sheets on top of each other, separated with a sheet of parchment to prevent sticking. Cover the half sheet pan with plastic wrap and place it in the fridge until the dough is cool to the touch and firm, 30 to 60 minutes.

CUTTING THE DOUGH

While the dough is chilling, prepare the stencil. Trace the stencil shape onto parchment paper, then cut it out with sharp scissors. Spray both sides of the stencil with nonstick spray; this will help it to stick to the dough while you are cutting, preventing dents caused by pressing and holding the stencil while cutting.

When the dough is chilled and ready to be cut, place the stencil over the dough and, using an X-ACTO® knife or other crafting blade positioned at a 90° angle, slowly begin to run the blade around the outside of the stencil. Be sure to go slowly and keep the blade at a 90° angle; this will give you the cleanest lines. If the dough starts to warm up, you will notice it start to tear; re-chill until firm to the touch.

SMOOTHING BUTTERCREAM

Smoothing buttercream takes a little practice but there are some tools and techniques you can use to get the process right. I recommend using a small offset spatula that has been slightly heated in a glass of warm water. The heat will help slightly melt the frosting to make spreading easier. As you work, rewet the spatula often and remove any excess frosting that may build up as you are smoothing the surface. The spatula should always be slightly wet; the water will help with the smoothing process.

I suggest smoothing the buttercream on all the cookies you'll be decorating at once so you don't need to reheat the water between cookies.

TOOLS AND EQUIPMENT

KITCHEN SCALE

Nothing is more important in baking than accuracy, and a scale will offer this. When using a scale, weigh the ingredients directly into the mixing bowl, zeroing the scale out between ingredients. When scaling directly into the mixing bowl, it is important to go slow so that you allow the scale to register and accurately read, and to avoid having to adjust for overmeasuring. Using a kitchen scale may seem intimidating at first, but it has many benefits. A cup of anything never weighs the same twice, and some of the ingredient is often left in the measuring cup, producing waste. Scaling will provide consistency in your results and will cut your prep and clean-up time.

ROLLING PIN

A good wooden rolling pin is an essential piece of equipment in the cookie decorating kitchen. The best rolling pin is the one that feels right in your hands and one that you find easy to control. Everyone has one style they prefer above all others and for reasons that are usually personal.

SILICONE GUIDE BANDS/RINGS

Silicone guides bands or rings that slip over the ends of the rolling pin help you roll your dough out to an even surface effortlessly. The guide bands come in five thicknesses ranging from 1/16 inch (1.5 mm) to 1/2 inch (13 mm). These guides are great for getting consistency both in the look of your cookies and with bake time. The thicker the cookie, the longer the bake time, so if you have a mix of thick and thin consistencies on the same baking sheet, some will be overdone while others may be a little underdone.

NON-STICK BAKING MAT

A heat-resistant silicone mat, such as a Silpat®, can be a great alternative to parchment paper. The silicon mat not only provides a great reusable non-stick surface for baking but also provides a great surface for rolling and cutting (with cookie cutters only; mats are not self-healing) cookie shapes.

PARCHMENT PAPER

A heat-resistant, non-stick paper can be used to line baking sheets and can also be used for rolling and cutting cookie dough. Sheets of parchment can be used two to three times, making them somewhat reusable, but you can also toss them when baking is finished, making for quick and easy clean-up.

FLEXIBLE SPATULAS

A thin, sturdy metal spatula is often hard to come by, so when you find one, buy two! One of my favorites is the Ateco 1352 stainless-steel cookie spatula. Available for roughly $5 each, these flexible metal spatulas are worth every penny.

OFFSET METAL SPATULAS

Having a few small offset metal spatulas on hand is a must. These spatulas are super versatile and always in use when working with buttercream. They can be used to apply buttercream to cookies, they work wonders when smoothing out buttercream and they offer a lot of control when working with smaller cookies and cakes.

OVEN THERMOMETER

I have had the pleasure of using one or two ovens that are actually accurate in temperature. That being said, oven temperature is critical to your baked goods being baked properly, so investing in an oven thermometer is well worth the money. They can be found in most well-stocked kitchen supply stores or online.

PIPING BAGS

Piping bags are available in many shapes, sizes and price ranges. The bag I choose depends on the task: For smaller detailed piping, I choose tipples bags; for larger tasks with specialty tips, I tend to go with either a disposable plastic bag or a reusable cloth bag from Ateco.

PIPING TIPS

A good selection of piping tips can make design work effortless and more creative. Most tips are available at well-stocked kitchen stores and online for under $1 each. You will find specific notes on the piping tips you will need throughout the projects.

STAND MIXER

The mixing speeds and timing used in this book are based on using a stand mixer. If you want to use a handheld mixer, that will also work very well. It will just take a little extra time, so you will need to adjust accordingly, paying close attention to what the product is doing and the recipe is telling you.

FINE-MESH SIEVE

A fine-mesh sieve can be used for anything from refining pastry cream and removing pulp from citrus juices, to incorporating dry ingredients and removing lumps. A medium to large size can be a great investment for any kitchen.

RASP GRATER

A stainless-steel grater can be used for grating whole nutmeg, fresh aromatic roots, hard cheeses and chocolates and is amazing for removing the zest of citrus fruits while leaving the bitter pith behind.

SELF-HEALING MAT

Self-healing mats are surprisingly useful in the kitchen. They are mostly non-stick and can be easily cleaned and sanitized. They will keep your blades from dulling and spare your countertops from scratches. They can be purchased at a craft or office supply store.

X-ACTO KNIFE

This small, pointed blade can be used for cutting intricate shapes with accuracy. X-Acto knives and replacement blades can be purchased at a craft or office supply store.

FOOD-GRADE PEN

Food-grade pens have been Food and Drug Administration (FDA)-approved for human consumption. They will be marked "food grade" and should not be confused with non-toxic pens which are *not* FDA-approved for human consumption. Food-grade pens are available at most craft and restaurant supply stores or can be purchased online. I have used these pens for many projects and highly recommend finding one to add to your decorating tool kit.

METAL SCRIBE

Metal scribes are fine-point metal tools with a plastic or wooden handle. They are useful for making reference points when food-grade markers are unavailable, they can be used to add small details to cookies and they are also very useful for clearing blocked piping tips. They can be purchased at most craft and restaurant supply stores.

ULTIMATE VANILLA SUGAR COOKIES

YIELD: 24 (3-INCH [7.5-CM]) COOKIES

Crisp on the outside, tender on the inside, and always bursting with buttery flavor, sugar cookies are a baker's go-to cookie. They are the ultimate versatile cookies—the dough can be rolled out for cutouts, chilled and sliced or used to make spritz cookies. This dough is versatile enough that you can mix in your favorite candies, cookies, sprinkles and flavors. Whatever your preference, they are sure to be a crowd pleaser.

---

1 cup (227 g) high-quality salted butter (at room temperature)

1 cup (200 g) granulated sugar

1 large egg (at room temperature)

2 tsp (10 ml) vanilla extract

3 cups (375 g) all-purpose flour, plus more for rolling

2 tbsp (16 g) cornstarch

In a large mixing bowl, cream the butter and sugar, scraping down the sides of the mixing bowl as needed. The butter and sugar should become light yellow when they are fully creamed together. Add the egg and mix again, scraping down the sides of the bowl. Add the vanilla extract and mix until completely incorporated, 1 to 2 minutes, scraping down the sides of the mixing bowl.

In a separate bowl, sift the flour and cornstarch. With the mixer on low, add the flour mixture to the butter mixture in three small batches. Mix until just combined, scraping down the sides of the bowl between batches.

Transfer the dough to a clean work surface. Divide the dough in half and shape each half into a flattened disk; wrap each disk in plastic wrap. Refrigerate the dough for at least 1 hour or overnight.

When you are ready to roll out and cut your cookies, refer to the Cookie Basics section on page 9.

Preheat the oven to 350°F (175ºC).

Bake the cookies, rotating the sheets halfway through, until the cookies are crisp and lightly golden at the edges, 10 to 15 minutes. Transfer the cookies to a wire rack to cool completely.

Cookies can be kept in an airtight container at room temperature for up to 5 days.

ALMOND BLISS SUGAR COOKIES

YIELD: 26 (3-INCH [7.5-CM]) COOKIES

This twist on the classic vanilla sugar cookie is my favorite. The addition of almond flour adds a crisp, nutty flavor that is punctuated by a hint of lemon zest. Plain or topped with buttercream, this cookie always hits the spot.

1½ cups (341 g) salted butter (at room temperature)

1 cup (200 g) granulated sugar

1 large egg (at room temperature)

1 tsp lemon zest

½ tsp almond extract

1 tsp vanilla extract

2 cups (190 g) almond flour

3 cups (375 g) all-purpose flour

In a large mixing bowl, cream the butter and sugar. The butter and sugar will become light yellow when they are fully creamed together.

Add the egg, lemon zest, almond extract and vanilla extract and mix until completely incorporated, scraping down the sides of the bowl as needed.

Add the almond flour, 1 cup (95 g) at a time, scraping down the sides of the bowl as needed.

In a separate bowl, sift the all-purpose flour. With the mixer on low, add the flour to the butter mixture in small batches. Mix until just combined.

Transfer the dough to a clean work surface. Divide the dough in half, shape each half into a flattened disk and wrap each disk in plastic wrap. Refrigerate the dough for at least 1 hour or overnight.

When you are ready to roll out and cut your cookies, refer to the Cookie Basics section on page 9.

Preheat the oven to 300°F (150°C).

Bake the cookies, rotating the sheets halfway through, until the cookies are crisp and lightly golden at the edges, 10 to 15 minutes. Transfer the cookies to a wire rack to cool completely.

Cookies can be kept in an airtight container at room temperature for up to 5 days.

AMERICAN BUTTERCREAM

American buttercream is the sweeter and less complicated cousin of the meringue buttercreams (Swiss, Italian and French). It holds color really well and is much stiffer than meringue buttercream, making it ideal for piping intricate designs in vibrant colors. American buttercream is most commonly flavored with vanilla, but is also delicious with almond, citrus or a berry puree for a naturally colored and flavored buttercream.

2 cups (454 g) salted butter (at room temperature)

5½ cups (660 g) powdered sugar (sifted)

¼ cup + 2 tbsp (89 ml) heavy whipping cream

2 tsp (10 ml) vanilla extract

In the bowl of a stand mixer fitted with the paddle attachment (or in a large bowl using a handheld mixer), cream the butter on medium speed for 2 to 3 minutes, until light and fluffy.

With the mixer on low, alternate between the wet and dry ingredients. Start by slowly adding about half of the powdered sugar, then add the heavy whipping cream and vanilla extract and finally add the remaining half of the powdered sugar. When the second half of sugar is incorporated, turn the mixer up to medium–high and mix for 3 to 5 minutes, or until the mixture is smooth and creamy.

Leftover buttercream can be stored in an airtight container in the fridge for up to 1 week and in the freezer for up to 3 months.

BUTTERCREAM COLOR GUIDE

Almost any baker you ask will tell you their favorite part of creating buttercream for cakes and cookies is color, and I am no exception. Color adds a layer of creativity, and the possibilities are literally endless. Adding color gives any baker the ability to personalize their confections. In this section, I will share with you some of my favorite buttercream colors and the products I use to make them.

I have been making buttercream for as long as I can remember. From the early days when I was very young baking with my grandmother to today, I have found there are many variations of buttercream and dyes, and it's helpful to know a little bit about how the dyes react with the ingredients. My recipe for American Buttercream (page 17) is higher in fat and lower in sugar, and for that reason I like to use oil-based food dye. I really love the colors produced by Colour Mill in recent years—they are vibrant and deep. Colour Mill also sells a large set of their oil-based colors, which can be a fun way to get acquainted with their color palettes. I mix their food dyes to produce the colors used in the tutorials throughout the book—I suggest you use them to get the best results.

Measuring food gel can be a bit tricky, especially for the smaller amounts required to achieve light tones. I find it helpful to measure onto a metal spatula with a dab of buttercream on it. For extra-small and ½ drops, I place a drop of food gel onto a plate and use a metal scribe to place the small amount onto the metal spatula. It is always a good idea to add less than more, as you can always make the buttercream darker. All of these recipes are scalable, too. Simply scale them up or down as you work through the projects if you need more or less of a color.

APPLE

½ cup (114 g) American Buttercream (page 17)

10 drops red Colour Mill food dye

1 drop brown Colour Mill food dye

Place the buttercream, red and brown food dye in a small mixing bowl. Mix well with a rubber spatula.

BLACK

½ cup (114 g) American Buttercream (page 17)

8 drops black Colour Mill food dye

Place the buttercream and black food dye in a small mixing bowl. Mix well with a rubber spatula.

BRICK

½ cup (114 g) American Buttercream (page 17)

12 drops red Colour Mill food dye

8 drops brown Colour Mill food dye

Place the buttercream, red and brown food dye in a small mixing bowl. Mix well with a rubber spatula.

CANARY YELLOW

½ cup (114 g) American Buttercream (page 17)

6 drops yellow Colour Mill food dye

Place the buttercream and yellow food dye in a small mixing bowl. Mix well with a rubber spatula.

CARAMEL

½ cup (114 g) American Buttercream (page 17)

4 drops clay Colour Mill food dye

1 drop orange Colour Mill food dye

2 drops yellow Colour Mill food dye

Place the buttercream, clay, orange and yellow food dye in a small mixing bowl. Mix well with a rubber spatula.

CERISE PINK

½ cup (114 g) American Buttercream (page 17)

2 drops burgundy Colour Mill food dye

Place the buttercream and burgundy food dye in a small mixing bowl. Mix well with a rubber spatula.

CINDER ROSE LIGHT

1 cup (227 g) American Buttercream (page 17)

2 drops blush Colour Mill food dye

1 extra-small drop burgundy Colour Mill food dye

Place the buttercream, blush and burgundy food dye in a small mixing bowl. Mix well with a rubber spatula.

CINDER ROSE MEDIUM

½ cup (114 g) American Buttercream (page 17)

2 drops blush Colour Mill food dye

1 extra-small drop burgundy Colour Mill food dye

Place the buttercream, blush and burgundy food dye in a small mixing bowl. Mix well with a rubber spatula.

CINDER ROSE DARK

½ cup (114 g) American Buttercream (page 17)

2 drops blush Colour Mill food dye

1 drop burgundy Colour Mill food dye

Place the buttercream, blush and burgundy food dye in a small mixing bowl. Mix well with a rubber spatula.

FLAMINGO PINK

½ cup (114 g) American Buttercream (page 17)

2 drops rose Colour Mill food dye

Place the buttercream and rose food dye in a small mixing bowl. Mix well with a rubber spatula.

GOLDEN CARROT

½ cup (114 g) American Buttercream (page 17)

4 drops caramel Colour Mill food dye

2 drops yellow Colour Mill food dye

1 drop orange Colour Mill food dye

Place the buttercream, caramel, yellow and orange food dye in a small mixing bowl. Mix well with a rubber spatula.

GREEN TEA

½ cup (114 g) American Buttercream (page 17)

2 drops mint Colour Mill food dye

Place the buttercream and mint food dye in a small mixing bowl. Mix well with a rubber spatula.

MAUVE LIGHT

1 cup (227 g) American Buttercream (page 17)

1 drop burgundy Colour Mill food dye

1 extra-small drop black Colour Mill food dye

Place the buttercream, burgundy and black food dye in a mixing bowl. Mix well with a rubber spatula.

MAUVE MEDIUM

½ cup (114 g) American Buttercream (page 17)

1 drop burgundy Colour Mill food dye

1 extra-small drop black Colour Mill food dye

Place the buttercream, burgundy and black food dye in a small mixing bowl. Mix well with a rubber spatula.

MAUVE DARK

½ cup (114 g) American Buttercream (page 17)

2 drops burgundy Colour Mill food dye

1 extra-small drop black Colour Mill food dye

Place the buttercream, burgundy and black food dye in a small mixing bowl. Mix well with a rubber spatula.

MOCHA

½ cup (114 g) American Buttercream (page 17)

10 drops chocolate Colour Mill food dye

Place the buttercream and chocolate food dye in a small mixing bowl. Mix well with a rubber spatula.

MOSS

½ cup (114 g) American Buttercream (page 17)

4 drops green Colour Mill food dye

4 drops yellow Colour Mill food dye

1 drop black Colour Mill food dye

Place the buttercream, green, yellow and black food dye in a small mixing bowl. Mix well with a rubber spatula.

PASTEL GREEN

½ cup (114 g) American Buttercream (page 17)

2 drops emerald Colour Mill food dye

Place the buttercream and emerald food dye in a small mixing bowl. Mix well with a rubber spatula.

PINE

½ cup (114 g) American Buttercream (page 17)

8 drops green Colour Mill food dye

1 drop midnight Colour Mill food dye

Place the buttercream, green and midnight food dye in a small mixing bowl. Mix well with a rubber spatula.

RUBY

½ cup (114 g) American Buttercream (page 17)

14 drops red Colour Mill food dye

2 drops brown Colour Mill food dye

Place the buttercream, red and brown food dye in a small mixing bowl. Mix well with a rubber spatula.

SWAN WING

½ cup (114 g) American Buttercream (page 17)

12 drops white Colour Mill food dye

Place the buttercream and white food dye in a small mixing bowl. Mix well with a rubber spatula.

TERRACOTTA

½ cup (114 g) American Buttercream (page 17)

5 drops rust Colour Mill food dye

Place the buttercream and rust food dye in a small mixing bowl. Mix well with a rubber spatula.

TIGER LILY

½ cup (114 g) American Buttercream (page 17)

5 drops orange Colour Mill food dye

3 drops clay Colour Mill food dye

Place the buttercream, orange and clay food dye in a small mixing bowl. Mix well with a rubber spatula.

VIOLET

½ cup (114 g) American Buttercream (page 17)

1 drop burgundy Colour Mill food dye

½ drop royal Colour Mill food dye

1 extra-small drop yellow Colour Mill food dye

Place the buttercream, burgundy, royal and yellow food dye in a small mixing bowl. Mix well with a rubber spatula.

VIOLET LIGHT

½ cup (114 g) American Buttercream (page 17)

1 small drop burgundy Colour Mill food dye

1 extra-small drop royal Colour Mill food dye

1 extra-small drop yellow Colour Mill food dye

Place the buttercream, burgundy, royal and yellow food dye in a small mixing bowl. Mix well with a rubber spatula.

BUTTERCREAM PIPING 101

Piping can be a bit intimidating but, like anything, practice and you will develop your skills. When I saw my grandmother pipe a perfect pink rose, my 6-year-old self had no idea how it was possible. I just knew it was pure magic. It took me some time to gain the skills that my grandmother had; she was truly gifted and made hundreds of cakes. I hope that the information contained in this section will help get you started on a lifelong love of piping buttercream. Each project walks you through the specific piping motions, but you can always refer to this as a refresher.

LINES AND WRITING

When piping lines or writing, I prefer a #1 or a #2 round tip, depending on how large the line or word is going to be. When doing this type of piping, hold the piping bag between 90° and 45°, wherever you feel most comfortable. Start with the piping tip parallel to the surface of the cookie. Gently apply continuous and even pressure as you lift up slightly, allowing the buttercream to fall to the surface of the cookie. Continue in this manner until your desired line or design is complete. Release pressure and pull the piping bag away.

LOOPS

When piping loops with a round tip, hold the piping bag at a 90° angle perpendicular to the cookie surface. Gently apply pressure on the piping bag as you move in a clockwise motion while lifting the piping tip up slightly, allowing the buttercream to fall to the surface of the cookie.

DOTS

When piping dots with a round tip, hold the piping bag at a 90° angle perpendicular to the cookie surface. Gently apply pressure on the piping bag until you have a small round ball of buttercream that is the desired size. Release the pressure and pull the piping bag away. The dots will have a peak on the top; this can be flattened using a small, slightly damp paintbrush.

BOWS

When piping a bow, I prefer to use either a #1 or #2 Wilton round tip, depending on the size of the bow. Holding the piping bag at a 90° angle with the tip perpendicular to the cookie surface, start the bow in the center where the two loops meet. Gently apply pressure as you lift slightly up and create a teardrop shape starting and ending at the same point. Repeat this step for the second loop. After you have created the loops, add the tails. Holding the piping bag at a 90° angle and with the tip perpendicular to the cookie surface, gently apply pressure as you lift slightly up, angling the line down and out. Release pressure and pull the piping bag away to end. Repeat this step on the opposite side. Last, create a small dot at the point where all four parts intersect. Hold the piping bag at a 90° angle with the tip of the piping bag perpendicular to the cookie surface. Gently apply pressure on the bag until you have formed a small, round ball of buttercream. The dot will have a peak on the top; this can be flattened using a small, slightly damp paintbrush.

ROSETTES

When piping a rosette, choose a star tip that reflects the size of the rosette you wish to pipe. For very small detail work, Wilton piping tips #13–18 work very well. For making rosettes that are up to 1 inch (2.5 cm), choose Wilton piping tips #20 or #32. For rosettes over 1 inch (2.5 cm), use Ateco piping tips #825, 828, 855, 856 and 865 or Wilton #6B or 8B.

To start the rosette, hold the piping bag at a 90° angle with the tip parallel to the cookie surface. Gently apply pressure and start in the center of the rosette, working your way outward counterclockwise in a tight spiral. To end the rosette, gently ease off the pressure to create a tail that will taper into the side of the rosette.

STARS

When piping stars with a star tip, hold the piping bag at a 90° angle parallel to the cookie surface. Gently apply pressure on the piping bag until you have a small, round ball of buttercream that is the desired size. Release pressure and pull the piping bag away to end.

SHELL BORDER

Holding the piping bag at a 45° angle, gently apply pressure to create a small, round dot of buttercream. When the desired size is achieved, gently release pressure as you drag the tip away, creating the tail of the shell. Repeat this technique, overlapping the tail of the previous shell.

RUFFLES

Hold the piping bag at a 45° angle with the Ateco #126k tip against the surface of the cookie and the rounded portion of the tip facing the direction you want the bottom of the ruffle to be (the thinner edge produces the ruffle effect). Gently apply pressure as you move the piping tip slightly up and down or side to side, depending on the positioning of the ruffle on the cookie surface. Release pressure and pull the piping bag away.

ROSES

Using a #10 round tip, pipe a small cone of frosting roughly ½ inch (13 mm) large. Next, switch the tip to a #104 petal tip, and with the narrow side of the tip pointing upward, pipe a petal of buttercream that wraps itself around the topmost portion of the cone.

Next, pipe the inner layer of three petals. Holding the piping bag at a 45° angle with the narrow side of the piping tip pointing upward and slightly inward, start at the base of the cone, gently applying pressure and piping a small arch that reaches slightly above the cone. Release pressure to end. Repeat this step two more times, slightly overlapping the arches.

For the outer layer of petals, hold the piping bag at a 45° angle with the narrow side of the piping tip facing upward and slightly outward. Starting at the base of the cone, gently apply pressure and pipe a small arch that reaches slightly above the cone. Release pressure to end. Repeat this step four more times, slightly overlapping the arches.

LEAVES

When making leaves, I have two tips that I almost always use: a #352 Ateco leaf piping tip and a #352 Wilton leaf piping tip. Hold the piping bag at a 45° angle with the open sides of the tip parallel to the surface of the cookie. Gently apply pressure to create the body of the leaf shape. When you have the desired shape and size, release pressure as you move in a downward motion to create the tip of the leaf.

LOVE AND APPRECIATION

If there is one thing I have learned over the past few years, it is to cherish the ones I love, count my blessings daily and let those near and dear to me know how truly loved they are. Food has been a big part of that love language for me. A special treat packed in a lunch or a box of hearts for a friend, there is never a bad time to remind the people in your life that they are loved. The cookies in this chapter are meant to remind us of just that.

PINK SCALLOPED HEARTS

YIELD: 53 (2-INCH [5-CM]) COOKIES

The symbol of the heart can be traced back to as early as the seventh century BC; it is rumored that the image of the heart is comprised of two human hearts coming together, making up the heart shape we have grown to identify as a symbol of love and affection. These simple little hearts are just that—a sweet little treat that can be made when time is limited and love abounds.

INGREDIENTS

1 batch Ultimate Vanilla Sugar Cookies (page 13)

1 batch American Buttercream (page 17), divided and dyed in the following amounts:

2 cups (454 g) cinder rose dark (page 20)

1½ cups (341 g) cinder rose medium (page 20)

1½ cups (341 g) cinder rose light (page 19)

SUPPLIES

Pink Scalloped Hearts template (page 131)

3 piping bags

3 #8B Wilton piping tips

Fine-point paintbrush

Edible gold leaf

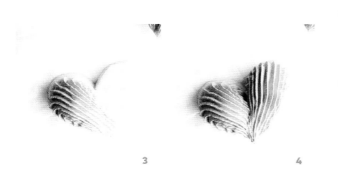

3   4

1. Prepare the sugar cookie dough. Cut the dough with the Pink Scalloped Hearts template and bake the cookies. Prepare the buttercream and measure it into small mixing bowls. Color the buttercream according to the Buttercream Color Guide (page 18).

2. Fill a piping bag fitted with a #8B Wilton piping tip with the cinder rose dark buttercream. Repeat this step for the cinder rose medium and cinder rose light buttercream.

3. First pipe one side of the heart. Choose any color to use first. I generally do one color at a time, and pipe one-third of the cookies with each color. Hold the piping bag at a 90° angle with the tip perpendicular to the surface of the cookie. Gently apply pressure while rotating the piping bag from a 90° starting point to a 140° angle at the bottom tip of the heart. To create a pointed tip, let off pressure roughly three-quarters of the way through the motion. This will allow for less buttercream to release and thus create the point.

4. Repeat step 3 on the opposite side of the heart cookie. Repeat steps 3 and 4 with the color of buttercream you chose and do the same for the two remaining colors. Refill the piping bags with buttercream as needed. Leftover buttercream can be stored in an airtight container in the fridge for up to 1 week and in the freezer for up to 3 months.

5. Using the fine-point paintbrush, gently pick up a small piece of gold leaf using only the tip of the brush. Gently place it on the top right corner of the heart.

6. Repeat step 5 with the remaining cookies.

CELEBRATION RIBBONS

YIELD: 14 (4-INCH [10-CM]) COOKIES

I first created this cookie for a busy mom who needed treats for the last day of Little League baseball. Not only were they a hit, but they became a repeat request from moms who wanted to celebrate the milestones, heroes and people special to them with a cookie that lets them know how amazing they are!

INGREDIENTS

1 batch Ultimate Vanilla Sugar Cookies (page 13)

1½ batches American Buttercream (page 17), divided and dyed in the following amounts:

1 cup (227 g) flamingo pink (page 20)

½ cup (114 g) black (page 19)

1 cup (227 g) cerise pink, divided (page 19)

1 cup (227 g) canary yellow (page 19)

1 cup (227 g) golden carrot, divided (page 20)

1 cup (227 g) pastel green (page 21)

1 cup (227 g) green tea, divided (page 20)

1 tsp light corn syrup

Nonstick cooking spray

SUPPLIES

Celebration Ribbons template (page 131)

Food-grade pen

10 piping bags

6 #126K Ateco piping tips

Small offset spatula

1 #1 Wilton piping tip

3 #27 Wilton piping tips

1. Prepare the sugar cookie dough. Cut the dough with the Celebration Ribbons template and bake the cookies. Prepare the buttercream and measure it out into small mixing bowls. Color the buttercream according to the Buttercream Color Guide (page 18).

2. Using a food-grade pen, draw a circle ½ inch (13 mm) from the border of the circular portion of the cookie.

3. Fill a piping bag fitted with a #126K Ateco piping tip with flamingo pink buttercream. Holding the piping bag at a 90° angle with the tip perpendicular to the cookie surface, gently apply pressure as you move in a zig-zag motion, releasing pressure once the circle is completely filled in.

4. With a small offset spatula, smooth out the body of the circle (see tips for smoothing buttercream in the Cookie Basics section on page 9).

5. Add the corn syrup to the black buttercream. Mix well. The addition of corn syrup will prevent the buttercream from breaking off and help it to flow smoothly as you are doing the lettering. Fill a piping bag fitted with a #1 Wilton piping tip with the black buttercream. Holding the piping bag at a 45° angle with the tip against the surface of the cookie, gently apply pressure as you lift up slightly, allowing the buttercream to fall to the cookie surface. I decided to use a variety of phrases for these ribbons, which you can use, or use them as inspiration to create your own messages. For practice, try writing "Great Job!" on a piece of parchment paper. I did the "great" in all caps, and the "job" in a lowercase cursive font. To get more specific tips on piping lettering, see page 23.

(continued)

6. Next, using the piping bag of flamingo pink fitted with a #126K Ateco piping tip, pipe two slightly overlapping inside ribbons. To create the first ribbon strand, hold the piping bag at a 45° angle against the surface of the cookie. Gently apply pressure as you slowly drag the piping tip across the surface of the cookie, creating one strip of buttercream on one strand of the ribbon. Repeat on the opposite side, slightly overlapping the first strand at the top.

7. Fill a piping bag fitted with a #126K Ateco piping tip with ½ cup (114 g) of the cerise pink buttercream. This will be used to make a second set of slightly overlapping strands of the ribbons. Hold the piping bag at a 45° angle against the surface of the cookie. Gently apply pressure as you slowly drag the piping tip across the surface of the cookie, slightly overlapping the flamingo pink strand. Repeat on the opposite side.

8. Using the piping bag of flamingo pink fitted with a #126K Ateco piping tip, pipe the ruffle around the circle of buttercream containing your message. Hold the piping bag at a 45° angle with the tip against the surface of the cookie and the rounded portion of the tip facing outward (the thinner edge produces the ruffle effect). Gently apply pressure as you move the piping tip slightly up and down to give the appearance of pleats. Continue to move around the circle until you have reached the starting point. Release pressure and pull away the piping bag to end.

9. Fill a piping bag fitted with a #27 Wilton piping tip with the remaining ½ cup (114 g) of cerise pink. This will be used to pipe the shell border along the inside edge of the ruffle. Holding the piping bag at a 45° angle, gently apply pressure to create a small, rounded dot of buttercream. Once the desired size is achieved (mine are about pea-sized), gently release pressure as you drag the tip away, creating the tail of the shell. Repeat this technique, overlapping the tail of the previous shell.

10. Repeat steps 2 through 9 with the remaining colors of buttercream, pairing canary yellow with golden carrot and pastel green with green tea. Use the black buttercream to pipe your message. You could say "Super star!" or "Best ever!"—or a saying of your choice! Refill the piping bags with buttercream as needed. Leftover buttercream can be stored in an airtight container in the fridge for up to 1 week and in the freezer for up to 3 months.

SPRINGTIME CELEBRATIONS

I always get excited about the changing of seasons. Spring in particular is very special when the days start to grow longer, when the birds start to sing again in the early morning light and nature begins anew. Using simple techniques, like rosettes, dots and lines, you can capture the themes of spring. You will also practice smoothing buttercream to create shapes and a flawless finish. And just like the beautiful colors of spring, these cookies are full of natural and pastel hues. You'll love the dainty and vibrant way they jump off a plate. The Cheery Chicks (page 41) are a great cookie to bring to a baby shower and the Blooming Tulips (page 48) make a great Mother's Day gift.

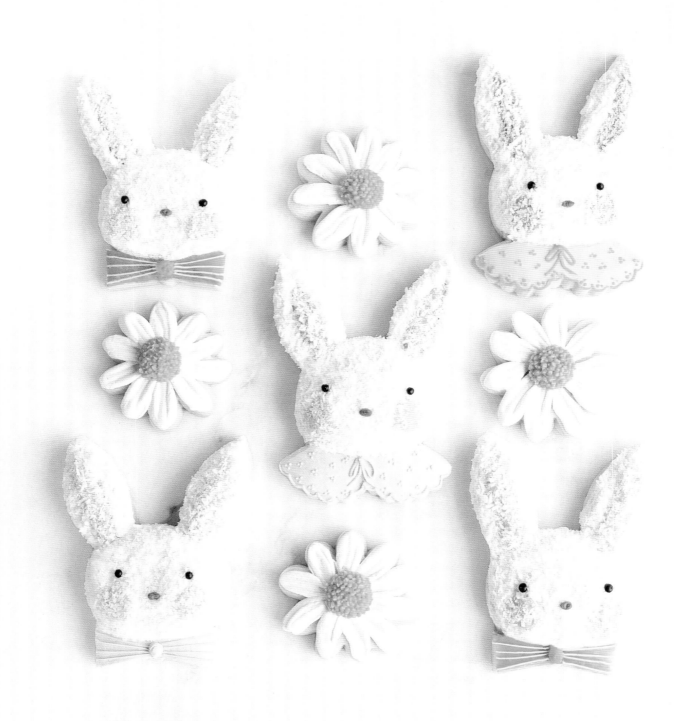

SPRINGTIME BUNNY BOYS AND GIRLS

YIELD: 12 (5-INCH [13-CM]) COOKIES

These cookies pull at the heartstrings of every childhood dream I ever had about bunnies. As an adult, I still have a fondness for their very image and the fables that have been told about them for hundreds of years. The flavors of vanilla bean and coconut topped with buttercream colored in the soft pastels of spring are perfect for an Easter basket or a day of spring baking with a loved one.

INGREDIENTS

1 batch Ultimate Vanilla Sugar Cookies (page 13)

1 batch American Buttercream (page 17), divided and dyed in the following amounts:

2 cups (454 g) swan wing (page 22)

½ cup (114 g) flamingo pink (page 20)

½ cup (114 g) black (page 19)

½ cup (114g) cerise pink (page 19)

½ cup (114g) green tea (page 20)

½ cup (114 g) golden carrot (page 20)

½ cup (114 g) canary yellow (page 19)

2 cups (186 g) shredded coconut

SUPPLIES

Springtime Bunny Boys and Girls templates (pages 131–132)

5 piping bags

4 #2 Wilton piping tips

2 #10 Wilton piping tips

Small offset spatula

2 tipless piping bags

1. Prepare the sugar cookie dough. Cut the dough with the Springtime Bunny Boys and Girls templates (pages 131–132) and bake. Prepare the buttercream and measure it into small mixing bowls. Color the buttercream according to the Buttercream Color Guide (page 18).

2. Fill a piping bag fitted with a #2 Wilton piping tip with the swan wing buttercream to make the outline of the bunny's face and ears. Starting at the outer edge of the cookie, hold the piping bag perpendicular to the cookie surface as you begin to apply continuous, even pressure. Lift up slightly as you go, letting the buttercream fall to the cookie surface. Continue until you have outlined the face and ears of the bunny cookie.

3. Change the swan wing piping bag from a #2 Wilton piping tip to a #10 Wilton piping tip to fill in the outlined areas. Place the tip of the piping bag perpendicular to the cookie surface. Beginning at the outer edge of the cookie, move in a circular motion, ending in the center of the face and creating a higher point in the center. Continue with the ears, moving in a zig-zag motion on the edges, leaving a slightly open space in the middle of each ear.

4. Fill a piping bag fitted with a #10 Wilton piping tip with the flamingo pink buttercream to fill in the center of the ears and give the bunny rosy cheeks. To pipe the cheeks, hold the tip of the piping bag at a 90° angle (pushing into the white frosting slightly) and apply a small amount of pressure until you have a dot the size of a pencil eraser. Next fill in the ears. Starting at the base, apply a small amount of pressure, gently releasing as you reach the tip of the ear.

(continued)

5. Continue filling all the cookies up to this step. Then, use a small offset spatula to smooth out the buttercream (see tips for smoothing buttercream in the Cookie Basics section on page 9). When smoothing the buttercream, you can add depth to the face by maintaining the rounded surface you created in the piping step. When all the cookies have been smoothed, sprinkle shredded coconut over the cookies by hand; this will maintain the shape of the frosting. (If you press the cookie into the coconut, it will create a flat surface and cause the buttercream to spread over the edges of the cookie.)

6. Fill a tipless piping bag with the black buttercream. With sharp scissors, cut a tiny amount off the tip of the bag to create a small hole capable of piping fine lines. Repeat this step if needed, until you have an opening that will pipe the details shown in the example photos. Fill a piping bag fitted with a #2 Wilton piping tip with the cerise pink buttercream. With the black buttercream, pipe the eyes of the bunny. Holding the piping bag slightly above the cheek at a 90° angle on the surface of the cookie, gently apply pressure until you have a small dot that looks proportionate. Repeat on the other side. Then, to make the nose, position the tip of the piping bag of cerise pink in the middle of the face and slightly lower than the eyes. Holding the bag at a 140° angle with the tip on the surface of the cookie, gently apply pressure while moving the tip slightly horizontally to create a small oval nose.

7. To make the bow ties, fill a piping bag fitted with a #2 Wilton piping tip with green tea buttercream and another fitted with a #2 Wilton piping tip with golden carrot buttercream. Start by outlining the area for the bow tie. I made two bow ties green and two yellow, but you can do what speaks to you! Holding the tip of the piping bag perpendicular to the cookie surface, gently apply pressure to form the outline. When finished with the outline, immediately fill in the area with a zig-zag motion.

8. Use a small offset spatula to smooth out the buttercream (see tips for smoothing buttercream in the Cookie Basics section on page 9).

9. Fill a tipless piping bag with canary yellow buttercream. Using sharp scissors, cut the tip the tiniest amount and test the line diameter. Adjust until you have achieved your desired line width. For the stripes on the bow ties, start in the center of the bowtie, holding the piping bag at a 140° angle, and gently apply pressure as you move toward the outer edge of the bow tie creating a line. Slowly release pressure to end the line. Repeat as necessary; I put three to four lines on each side of the bow tie. Finally, add a small dot of green tea buttercream using the piping bag fitted with a #2 Wilton piping tip.

10. For the lace collars, use the piping bag of green tea buttercream fitted with a #2 Wilton piping tip. Outline the area for the lace collar. If you want, you can also alternate the collar colors with the green tea and golden carrot. Holding the tip of the piping bag perpendicular to the cookie surface, gently apply pressure to form the outline. When finished with the outline, immediately fill in the area with a zig-zag motion.

11. Repeat step 8 to smooth out the lace collars.

12. For the lace detail, use the tipless piping bag of canary yellow buttercream. Holding the tip perpendicular to the cookie, outline the bottom scalloped edge. Loops can be a bit difficult, so be sure to take it slow. Remember to start out against the cookie surface and pull it slightly above the cookie, letting the line fall where you want it. Working away from the cookie will give you more control. Review my tips on piping loops and bows on page 23.

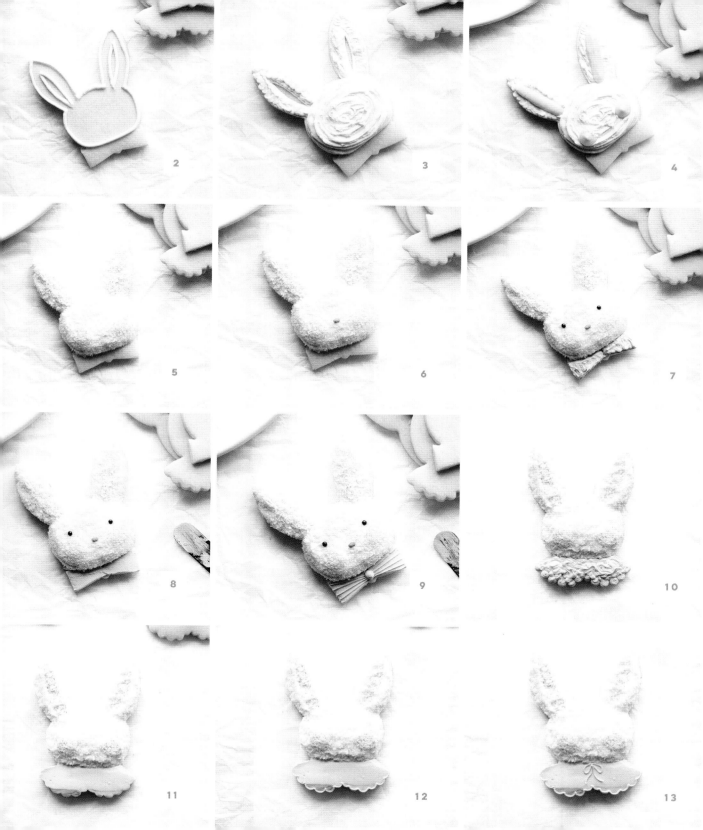

(continued)

13. To make the bow on the collar, hold the tipless piping bag of canary yellow buttercream at a 140° angle. Start in the center with the tip against the surface of the cookie and make the loops first. As you start to slowly apply pressure, lift slightly upward so the line is falling into place as you form the loops. The trailing ends are piped in the same way. Start in the center and hold the bag at a 140° angle with the tip against the surface of the cookie, then slowly apply pressure as you gently lift away from the cookie, letting the line fall.

14. Last, using the canary yellow buttercream, add dot clusters to give the look of eyelet lace. Holding the tipless piping bag at a 90° angle to the cookie surface, slowly apply pressure to create tiny dots, releasing pressure once you have achieved the size of dot you desire.

15. Repeat steps 6 through 14 with the remaining cookies. Refill the piping bags with buttercream as needed. Leftover buttercream can be stored in an airtight container in the fridge for up to 1 week and in the freezer for up to 3 months.

CHEERY CHICKS

These sweet little chicks are the perfect pairing for any spring basket of cookies. Their brightly colored yellow feathers are bursting with springtime colors and happy vibes.

INGREDIENTS

1 batch Ultimate Vanilla Sugar Cookies (page 13)

1 batch American Buttercream (page 17), divided and dyed in the following amounts:

2 cups (454 g) canary yellow (page 19)

½ cup (114 g) flamingo pink (page 20)

½ cup (114 g) violet light (page 22)

1 cup (227 g) pine (page 21)

½ cup (114 g) tiger lily (page 22)

½ cup (114 g) black (page 19)

1 cup (200 g) granulated sugar

SUPPLIES

Cheery Chicks template (page 132)

3 piping bags

2 #10 Wilton piping tips

Small offset spatula

Plate or bowl

2 #1 Wilton piping tips

1 #16 Ateco piping tip

3 tipless piping bags

1 #32 Ateco piping tip

1. Prepare the sugar cookie dough. Cut the dough with the Cheery Chicks template (page 132) and bake the cookies. Prepare the buttercream and measure it into small mixing bowls. Color the buttercream according to the Buttercream Color Guide (page 18).

2. Fill a piping bag fitted with a #10 Wilton piping tip with the canary yellow buttercream for the chick's body.

3. Hold the piping bag at a 90° angle on the outer edge of a cookie. Starting with the tip perpendicular to the surface of the cookie, slowly apply pressure as you move the tip upward, letting the buttercream fall on the cookie edge. Continue piping the outline until you reach the starting point and slowly release pressure to end the outline. Only outline the main body, not the feet.

4. With the same piping bag of canary yellow buttercream, fill in the body of the chick. This can be done in one of two ways. The first is to put down a single layer of buttercream. Holding the piping bag at a 140° angle, gently apply pressure as you move in a zig-zag motion to fill in the entire outline of the chick. The second option is to put the single layer of buttercream in a zig-zag motion, then go back and add additional layers. This creates a 3-D effect by building the face and body of the chick into a dome.

5. Use a small offset spatula to smooth out the surface of the buttercream (see tips for smoothing buttercream in the Cookie Basics section on page 9). If you haven't filled in the body of all the cookies yet, do so now and smooth them all out at once.

(continued)

6. Fill a piping bag fitted with a #10 Wilton piping tip with the flamingo pink buttercream to create the cheek of the chick. Position the cheek just to the right of the beak. Holding the piping bag at a 90° angle with the tip pressed slightly into the canary yellow buttercream, gently apply pressure until you have a small domed cheek. Smooth out the cheek without losing the round shape by heating up the offset spatula and gently pressing into the cheek area until it becomes flush with the rest of the chick's body.

7. Coat the body of the chick with a dusting of granulated sugar. Hold the cookie over a plate or bowl and sprinkle the sugar generously onto the cookie, letting the excess fall into the bowl or plate. (Don't press the cookie into the sugar, as that will cause the buttercream to flatten and spread out over the edge of the cookie.)

8. Change the tip of the bag of flamingo pink buttercream from the #10 Wilton piping tip to the #1 Wilton piping tip. Starting at the chick's neck to begin piping the bow, place the tip of the piping bag against the edge of the cookie. Slowly apply pressure to the piping bag as you lift up and guide the line along the base of the neck, lowering the tip as you release pressure to end the line. Next, to add the loops of the bow, place the tip of the piping bag against the line you just piped, about one-third of the way from the left edge of the line. Slowly apply pressure as you lift up on the piping bag and create a loop starting and ending at the same one-third mark. Repeat for the second loop. To add the ribbon ends, place the tip of the piping bag in the center of the two loops where they meet the line. Slowly apply pressure and lift up as you guide the line in a downward swooping motion, releasing pressure to end the line. Repeat for the second ribbon end. Review my tips on piping loops and bows on page 23.

9. Fill a piping bag fitted with an Ateco #16 piping tip with the violet light buttercream to create the rosette. Starting on the line just above the bow and holding the piping bag at a 90° angle, begin to slowly add pressure as you move the piping tip in a counter-clockwise motion, then gently release pressure to end the rosette. See page 24 for more tips on piping rosettes.

10. Fill a tipless piping bag with the pine buttercream to make the leaves. Hold the piping bag at a 40° angle with the tip of the bag on the surface of the cookie and as close to the flower as possible. Apply pressure slowly and create a small mound of frosting, then start to ease off the pressure as you pull upward, creating the middle and tip of the leaf.

11. Change the tip on the piping bag of canary yellow buttercream from the #10 Wilton piping tip to the #32 Ateco piping tip to pipe the wing. Starting just below the bow and rosette, hold the piping bag at a 40° angle against the surface of the cookie. Slowly apply pressure and begin slightly lifting and turning the bag at a 90° angle. As you release pressure, pull upward to create the end of the wing, ending just below the tail feathers with the piping bag at a 140° angle. When the wing is piped, give it a light dusting of granulated sugar using the same technique as in step 7.

12. Fill a tipless piping bag with the tiger lily buttercream to make the beak and feet. Using sharp scissors, cut the tip of the bag a tiny amount and test the line diameter. Adjust the size of the cut until you have achieved the desired line width. To make the legs, hold the piping bag at a 90° angle with the tip against the surface of the cookie and positioned at one of the two peaks at the bottom-most point of the cookie. Pipe one thin line for each leg. Add the toes to each leg by starting to pipe from the outer edge, to the mid-point on the leg and then down to the middle of the peaks. Repeat for the second leg.

(continued)

13. Using the same tipless bag of tiger lily buttercream, make the beak. Hold the tip of the piping bag at a 140° angle perpendicular to the body of the chick. Slowly apply pressure as you move in a slight zig-zag motion, creating a pyramid shape. As you reach the tip of the beak, slowly reduce pressure to end the design.

14. Fill a tipless piping bag or a piping bag fitted with a #1 Wilton piping tip with black buttercream. Position the tip of the piping bag just above the cheek. Apply pressure slowly until you have a dot that looks proportionate for an eye.

15. Repeat steps 2 through 14 with the remaining cookies. Refill the piping bags with buttercream as needed. Leftover buttercream can be stored in an airtight container in the fridge for up to 1 week and in the freezer for up to 3 months.

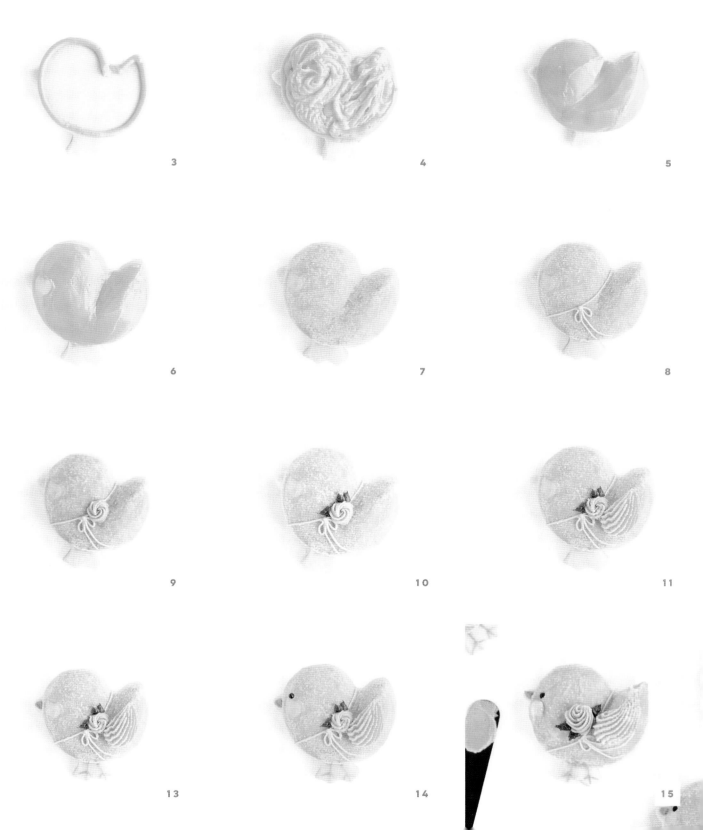

3

4

5

6

7

8

9

10

11

13

14

15

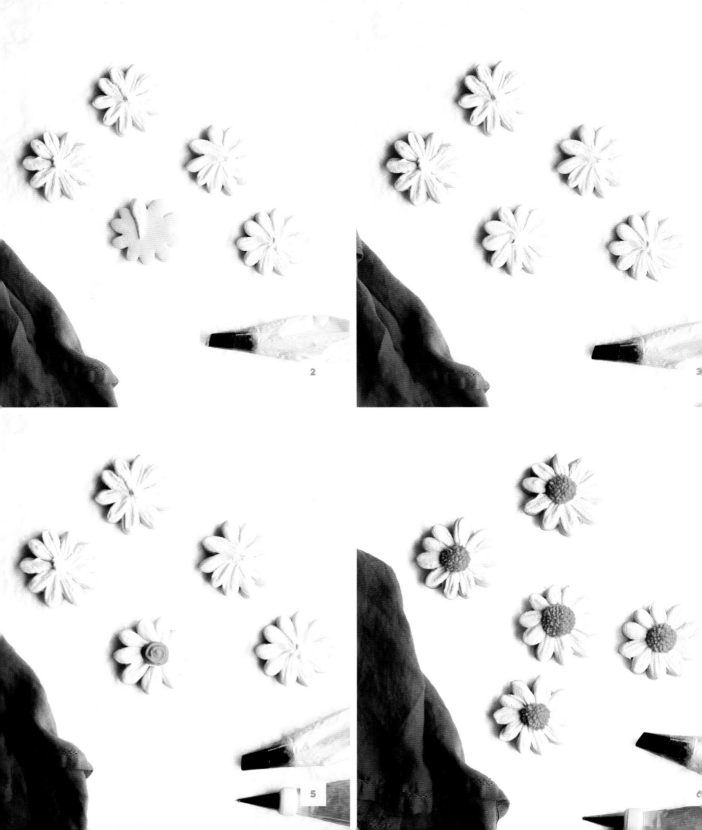

DAINTY DAISIES

Daisies are often overlooked, but I think they are such a happy little flower. To create a little two-bite sweet treat, it seemed like the perfect pairing to serve these daisies alongside the Springtime Bunny Boys and Girls. These cookies are also perfect on their own, tucked into a spring- or summer-themed basket of cookies or added to a Valentine's Day gift.

INGREDIENTS

1 batch Ultimate Vanilla Sugar Cookies (page 13)

½ batch American Buttercream (page 17), divided and dyed in the following amounts:

1½ cups (341 g) swan wing (page 22)

1 cup (227 g) golden carrot (page 20)

SUPPLIES

Dainty Daisies template (page 132)

2 piping bags

1 #104 Wilton piping tip

1 #2 Wilton piping tip

1. Prepare the sugar cookie dough. Cut the dough with the Dainty Daisies template (page 132) and bake the cookies. Prepare the buttercream and measure it into small mixing bowls. Color the buttercream according to the Buttercream Color Guide (page 18).

2. Fill a piping bag fitted with a #104 Wilton piping tip with the swan wing buttercream to pipe the daisy petals. Hold the wider end of the tip closest to you with the thin end at the top of the petal, keeping it perpendicular to the cookie surface. Start by applying pressure to create the wider part of the petal and gently let up on the pressure as you drag the tip toward the center of the cookie.

3. Repeat this step for each petal of all the cookies.

4. Fill a piping bag fitted with a #2 Wilton piping tip with the golden carrot buttercream to create the center of the daisy. Starting in the center of the cookie with the tip of the piping bag perpendicular to the cookie surface, apply pressure as you gently lift up, allowing the buttercream to fall to the cookie surface and creating the outline for the center.

5. Using the same piping bag of golden carrot buttercream, fill in the outline. Starting in the center of the outline, gently apply pressure as you move the tip in a circular motion until you have reached the outer edge.

6. Using the same piping bag of golden carrot buttercream, hold the tip against the outer edge of the large dot you piped and slowly apply pressure until you have created a small dot, then gently release pressure and lift up and away to finish the dot. Repeat this step, working form the outer edge inward, until you have covered the entire center with dots.

7. Repeat steps 2 through 6 with the remaining cookies. Refill the piping bags with buttercream as needed. Leftover buttercream can be stored in an airtight container in the fridge for up to 1 week and in the freezer for up to 3 months.

BLOOMING TULIPS

YIELD: 28 (3½-INCH [9-CM]) COOKIES

Traditionally, tulips are a flower that is given to show perfect and deep love, with yellow to declare you are "hopelessly in love," red as a "declaration of love" and pink to show "caring." For me, tulips are the official flower of spring. After a gray winter in the Pacific Northwest, their vibrant blooms are a symbol of love and sunny days to come. In this beautiful design, we will be playing with tones and practicing piping smooth edges. This design is all about the small details, so take your time as you move through it.

INGREDIENTS

1 batch Almond Bliss Sugar Cookies (page 14)

1 batch American Buttercream (page 17), divided and dyed in the following amounts:

1 cup (227 g) pine (page 21)

2 cups (454 g) violet (page 22)

2 cups (454 g) violet light (page 22)

SUPPLIES

Blooming Tulips template (page 132)

3 piping bags

3 #2 Wilton piping tips

Small offset spatula

1. Prepare the sugar cookie dough. Cut the dough with the Blooming Tulips template (page 132) and bake the cookies. Prepare the buttercream and measure it into small mixing bowls. Color the buttercream according to the Buttercream Color Guide (page 18).

2. Fill a piping bag fitted with a #2 Wilton piping tip with the pine buttercream to make the outline of the leaves. Place the tip of the piping bag perpendicular to the cookie surface. Start on the lower edge in the middle of the two leaves and move up to the point of the right leaf and then back to the center. Repeat this for the left leaf.

3. Using the same piping bag of pine fitted with a #2 Wilton piping tip, begin filling in the leaves. Start at the tip of the leaf and move toward the bottom in a zig-zag motion.

4. Using the small offset spatula slightly warmed in a glass of water, begin to smooth out the surface of the leaves (see tips for smoothing buttercream in the Cookie Basics section on page 9).

5. Fill a piping bag fitted with a #2 Wilton piping tip with the violet buttercream. Fill a second piping bag fitted with a #2 Wilton piping tip with the violet light buttercream. You will make flowers in both shades, so you can alternate between the colors at your choosing. Each tulip will use all of one shade or the other, so make sure to work with the same color for each cookie. Pipe the outline of the tulip by holding the tip of the piping bag perpendicular to the cookie surface. Slowly apply pressure as you lift up slightly, letting the buttercream fall into place.

(continued)

6. Using the same piping bag of either violet or violet light buttercream fitted with a #2 Wilton piping tip, fill in the tulips. Start at the top of the tulip and move toward the bottom in a zig-zag motion.

7. Using the small offset spatula, smooth out the surface of the tulip.

8. Using the piping bag with the same color used for the first layer, pipe the next petal of the tulip. It should cover two thirds of the main body and follow the dip in the top of the flower. Place the tip of the piping bag against the surface of the cookie at the top of the right petal and slowly apply pressure as you lift slightly, allowing the buttercream to fall into place. Continue to move toward the center tip, then toward the bottom and back to the starting point.

9. Fill in the tulip petal. Use the same color you used for the main body. Start at the top of the petal and move toward the bottom in a zig-zag motion.

10. Using the small offset spatula, smooth out the surface of the tulip petal.

11. Add a third petal, covering half of the right-hand side of the petal you piped in step 9. Using the piping bag with the same color, pipe the next petal of the tulip. Place the tip of the piping bag against the surface of the cookie at the top of the right petal and slowly apply pressure as you lift slightly, allowing the buttercream to fall into place. Continue to move toward the next tip, then toward the bottom and back to the start point. Then begin to fill in the tulip petal. Start at the top of the petal and move toward the bottom in a zig-zag motion.

12. Using the small offset spatula, smooth out the surface of the tulip petal.

13. Using the piping bag of pine buttercream, pipe the stem. Place the tip of the piping bag against the surface of the cookie at the center of the lower edge of the tulip. Move in a slight zig-zag motion as you slowly apply pressure, tapering the motion on the second zig-zag and moving straight down to the center point where the two leaves adjoin.

14. Use the piping bag of pine buttercream to pipe the veins of the leaves. Starting at the top point of the leaf, place the tip of the piping bag against the surface of the cookie and slowly apply pressure as you lift up slightly, allowing the buttercream to fall to the cookie surface. Repeat two to three times on each leaf.

15. Repeat steps 2 through 14 with the remaining cookies. Refill the piping bags with buttercream as needed. Leftover buttercream can be stored in an airtight container in the fridge for up to 1 week and in the freezer for up to 3 months.

DAZZLING DESERT DESIGNS

My love and respect for the desert and all that can survive its intense conditions runs deep. In my many trips to these seemingly uninhabitable places, I have seen more beauty than I could possibly tell you about. Arches made of vibrant terracotta-colored stone look like bridges to the bluest skies you could imagine. Cacti appear in all their glorious colors of greens, pinks, purples, reds and blues. Quiet moments in the early morning when the sun just begins to rise feature small creatures that can be seen making their way back to their shelter from the intense heat that is slowly creeping in. The desert is a magical place to become inspired. In this chapter, I hope to share some of that beauty with you. You'll use basic tips to create magnificent blooming cacti (page 64) and practice smoothing techniques and piping basic lines to create spectacular wildflowers (page 71) of the desert.

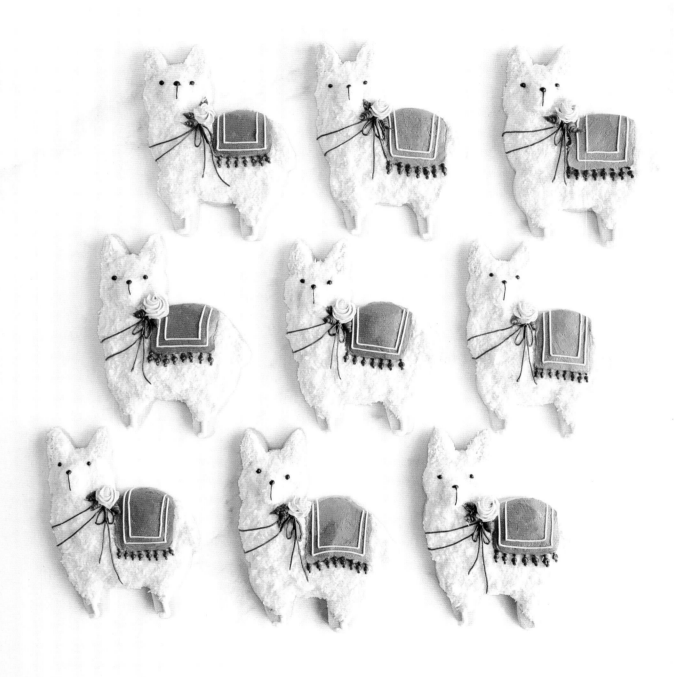

LOVELY LITTLE LLAMAS

YIELD: 12 (5-INCH [13-CM]) COOKIES

What could be more fun than a fuzzy llama? They are one of those magical creatures that spark joy and imagination in young and old alike. Using the smoothing technique, rosettes, lines and dots, you will be able to create these sweet little buttercream and coconut treats.

INGREDIENTS

1 batch Ultimate Vanilla Sugar Cookies (page 13)

1½ batches American Buttercream (page 17), divided and dyed in the following amounts:

3 cups (681 g) swan wing (page 22)

1 cup (227 g) flamingo pink, divided (page 20)

1½ cups (341 g) terracotta (page 22)

½ cup (114 g) brick (page 19)

½ cup (114 g) pine (page 21)

½ cup (114 g) black (page 19)

2 cups (186 g) shredded coconut

SUPPLIES

Lovely Little Llamas template (page 133)

7 piping bags

3 #2 Wilton piping tips

2 #10 Wilton piping tips

Small plate or bowl

Small offset spatula

2 #1 Wilton piping tips

1 #21 Wilton piping tip

1 tipless piping bag

1. Prepare the sugar cookie dough. Cut the dough with the Lovely Little Llamas template (page 133) and bake the cookies. Prepare the buttercream and measure it into small mixing bowls. Color the buttercream according to the Buttercream Color Guide (page 18).

2. Fill a piping bag fitted with a #2 Wilton piping tip with the swan wing buttercream to create the outline for the fur, omitting the area for the blanket. Holding the piping bag at a 90° angle with the tip of the piping bag against the surface of the cookie, slowly apply pressure as you lift up slightly, letting the line fall on the surface of the cookie.

3. When the outline is complete, switch the tip on the bag to a #10 Wilton piping tip and begin to fill in the llama. Holding the piping bag at a 90° angle with the tip against the surface of the cookie, slowly apply pressure to the piping bag while moving in a circular, wavy motion. Continue until the outline is completely filled in. Refill the piping bag with the swan wing buttercream as needed.

4. Fill a piping bag fitted with a #2 Wilton piping tip with ½ cup (114 g) of the flamingo pink buttercream. Holding the bag at a 90° angle with the tip against the surface of the cookie, slowly apply pressure while you move the tip in a circular, wavy motion. Begin at the tip of the ear and only fill in the outer half. Continue until the outer section of the ears are filled in.

5. Holding the iced cookie over a plate or bowl, sprinkle shredded coconut by hand over the cookie, being sure to coat the llama evenly. Tap the cookie gently to release any excess coconut.

(continued)

6. Using the piping bag of swan wing buttercream fitted with the #10 Wilton piping tip, pipe a raised oval for the snout of the llama. Position the tip of the piping bag at a 90° angle. Gently apply pressure to create the outline of the oval and immediately begin to fill in the oval to create a raised oval shape.

7. Repeat step 5 to cover the snout with shredded coconut.

8. Fill a piping bag fitted with a #10 Wilton piping tip with the terracotta buttercream to create the blanket. Holding the tip of the piping bag at a 90° angle against the surface of the cookie, gently apply pressure, moving in a zig-zag motion. Continue filling in the area for the blanket until it is the same height, or a tiny bit higher than, the fur of the llama. Refill the piping bag with terracotta buttercream as needed.

9. Using a small offset spatula, smooth out the surface of the blanket (see tips for smoothing buttercream in the Cookie Basics section on page 9).

10. Fill a piping bag fitted with a #1 Wilton piping tip with the brick buttercream to pipe the ribbon around the neck of the llama. Place the tip of the piping bag against the cookie surface at the base of the neck where it meets the back of the llama. Gently apply pressure as you lift up slightly, allowing the buttercream to fall into place. Slowly release pressure to end the line. Repeat the line, starting in the same place but ending it lower to create the double line look.

11. To pipe the bow, using the same bag of brick buttercream, slowly apply pressure as you lift up on the piping bag and create a loop starting and ending at the same mark. Repeat for the second loop. To add the ribbon ends, place the tip of the piping bag in the center of the two loops where they meet. Slowly apply pressure and lift up as you guide the line in a downward, swooping motion, releasing pressure to end the line. Repeat for the second ribbon end. Review my tips on piping loops and bows on page 23.

12. Fill a piping bag fitted with a #21 Wilson piping tip with flamingo pink buttercream. Create a rosette just to the right of the bow. Review the process for piping a rosette on page 24.

13. Fill a piping bag fitted with a #1 Wilton piping tip with the pine buttercream to make the leaves. Position the tip of the piping bag at a 45° angle against the surface of the cookie. Gently apply pressure to create the wider base of the leaf, then slowly move the piping bag horizontally away from the base of the leaf, reducing pressure to end the leaf. Repeat this process, creating two or three leaves around the rosette.

14. Use the piping bag with the brick buttercream to make the tassels. Start the tassels by holding the piping bag at a 90° angle, gently applying pressure to create small dots. Evenly space them along the bottom edge of the blanket. Repeat this process, adding a second row of dots that is slightly larger directly underneath the first row. Repeat a third time, adding a dot that is roughly the same size as the first row directly underneath the second row.

15. Change the tip on the piping bag of swan wing buttercream to a #2 Wilton piping tip to create the feet. The feet should look like a backward "L." Starting at the bottom left corner of the leg, place the tip of the piping bag at a 140° angle with the tip against the surface of the cookie. Slowly apply pressure to the piping bag as you move upward slightly and toward the middle of the leg. In the middle of the leg, gently tap the frosting down against the surface of the cookie and turn the piping bag to a 90° angle. Move upward toward the fur of the llama, easing off pressure to end the line when you reach the fur.

(continued)

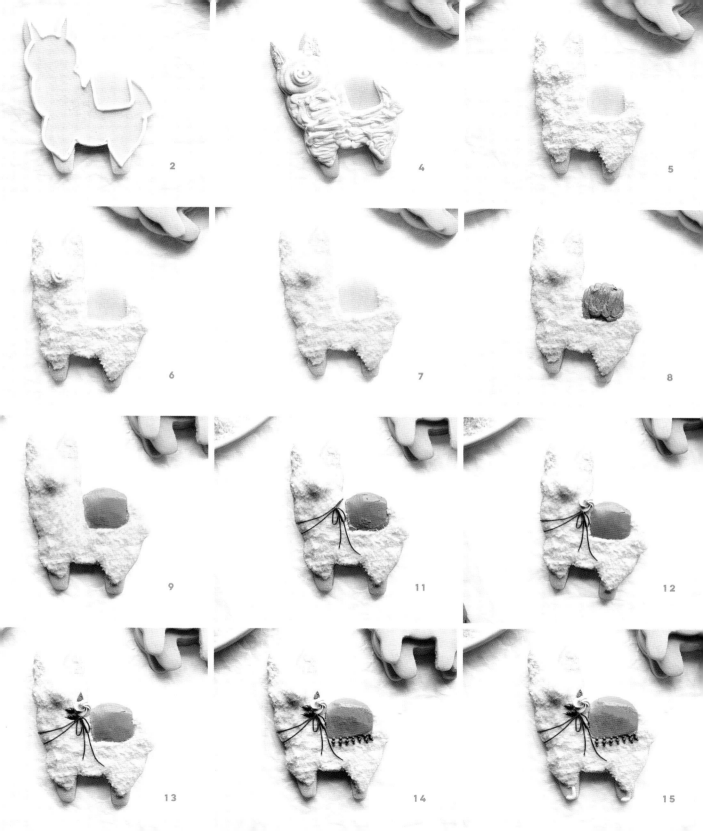

16. Fill a tipless piping bag with the black buttercream to create the details on the face of the llama. Using sharp scissors, cut a tiny amount off the tip and test the line diameter. Adjust the size of the cut until you have achieved the desired line width. For the nose, place the tip of the piping bag at the top middle portion of the muzzle and pipe a dot before adding a line descending from it to the bottom of the muzzle. Pipe dots for eyes last to help with balance and placement.

17. Change the tip on the piping bag of swan wing buttercream to a #1 Wilton tip to create the line design on the blanket. Place the tip of the piping bag on the left edge of the blanket. Gently apply pressure as you lift up slightly, allowing the buttercream to fall into place. Slowly release pressure to end the line. Repeat to create multiple lines.

18. Repeat steps 2 through 16 with the remaining cookies. Refill the piping bags with buttercream as needed. Leftover buttercream can be stored in an airtight container in the fridge for up to 1 week and in the freezer for up to 3 months.

CHOLLA MINIS

Cholla Minis are a staple in my list of cookies that I can make quickly as a sweet gift for any summer party. They are a perfect two-bite cookie iced with a sweet vanilla buttercream. In this tutorial, I use the same three piping tips to make three different designs, keeping it easy for you.

INGREDIENTS

1 batch Ultimate Vanilla Sugar Cookies (page 13)

1 batch American Buttercream (page 17), divided and dyed in the following amounts:

2 cups (454 g) moss (page 21)

2 cups (454 g) pine (page 21)

1 cup (227 g) cinder rose light (page 19)

SUPPLIES

Cholla Minis template (page 133)

3 piping bags

2 #32 Wilton piping tips

1 #8B Wilton piping tip

CHOLLA MINI ONE

1. Prepare the sugar cookie dough. Cut the dough with the Cholla Minis template (page 133) and bake the cookies. Prepare the buttercream and measure it into small mixing bowls. Color the buttercream according to the Buttercream Color Guide (page 18).

2. Fill a piping bag fitted with a #32 Wilton piping tip with the moss buttercream. Starting on the left side of the cookie, hold the piping bag at a 90° angle with the tip against the surface of the cookie. Gently apply pressure until you have a small dome of buttercream, then begin to pull upward as you release pressure, making a small dome shape. Repeat until you have covered the left side of the cookie with small domes.

3. Fill a piping bag fitted with a #8B Wilton piping tip with the pine buttercream. Starting in the upper middle section of the cookie, holding the piping bag a 90° angle with the tip against the surface of the cookie, gently apply pressure until you have a rounded area of buttercream that fills up at least half of the remaining space on the cookie.

4. Repeat step 3 on the remaining section of the cookie.

5. Fill a piping bag fitted with a #32 Wilton piping tip with the cinder rose light buttercream. Holding the tip of the piping bag in the middle of one of the pine domes, slowly apply pressure until you have a small dome of buttercream . Slowly reduce pressure as you pull upward, creating a peak and ending the design. Repeat on the other pine dome.

6. Repeat steps 1 through 4 with as many cookies you would like to do in this design. Refill the piping bags with buttercream as needed. Leftover buttercream can be stored in an airtight container in the fridge for up to 1 week and in the freezer for up to 3 months.

(continued)

2 A

2 B

3

3 B

4 A

4

5 A

5 B

5

7 A

7 B

7

8 A

8 B

8 C

9

10 A

10 B

12 A

12 B

12 C

12 D

12 E

13

CHOLLA MINI TWO

7. Using the piping bag of moss buttercream fitted with a #32 Wilton piping tip, starting in the middle of the cookie, hold the piping bag at a 90° angle with the tip against the surface of the cookie and gently apply pressure until you have a small dome of buttercream. Slowly reduce pressure as you pull upward, creating a peak and ending the design. Repeat until you have covered the top dome and middle section of the cookie with small domes.

8. Next, using the piping bag of pine fitted with a #8B Wilton piping tip, begin to fill in the sides of the cholla mini. Begin on the top-left section of the cookie. Holding the piping bag at a 90° angle with the tip against the surface of the cookie, begin to apply pressure until you have formed a small dome of buttercream (about the size of the rounded area of the cookie), then begin to drag the buttercream down the cookie, reducing pressure as you end the design.

9. Repeat step 8 on the right section of the cookie.

10. Use the piping bag of cinder rose light buttercream fitted with a #32 Wilton piping tip to pipe the flowers. Holding the tip of the piping bag against the upper-right edge of the cookie, gently apply pressure until you have formed a small dome of buttercream. Slowly reduce pressure as you pull upward, creating a peak and ending the design. Repeat this process on the left side of the cookie.

11. Repeat steps 7 through 10 with as many cookies you would like to do in this design. Refill the piping bags with buttercream as needed. Leftover buttercream can be stored in an airtight container in the fridge for up to 1 week and in the freezer for up to 3 months.

CHOLLA MINI THREE

12. Using the piping bag of pine fitted with a #8B Wilton piping tip, begin on the top-right section of the cookie. Holding the piping bag at a 90° angle with the tip against the surface of the cookie, begin to apply pressure until you have formed a small dome of buttercream (about the size of the rounded area of the cookie), then begin to drag the buttercream down the cookie, reducing the pressure as you end the design. Repeat this technique in the middle and left section of the cookie.

13. Use the piping bag of cinder rose light buttercream fitted with a #32 Wilton piping tip to pipe the flowers. Holding the tip of the piping bag against the upper right edge of the cookie, gently apply pressure until you have formed a small dome of buttercream. Slowly reduce the pressure as you pull upward, creating a peak and ending the design. Repeat this process on the middle and left side of the cookie.

14. Repeat steps 1 and 2 with as many cookies as you would like to do in this design. Refill the piping bags with buttercream as needed. Leftover buttercream can be stored in an airtight container in the fridge for up to 1 week and in the freezer for up to 3 months.

PRICKLY PEARS

YIELD: 22 (4-INCH [10-CM]) COOKIES

When I first saw these little cacti, I was so enamored by them. No two were alike and their colors were magical, ranging from green, pink, lavender, blue, brown and red. In this tutorial, I chose my favorite shades of green, blush and a beautiful terracotta to create my version of this beautiful cactus. I like to pair this design with my Cholla Minis (page 59). The green and earth tones go so well together!

INGREDIENTS

1 batch Ultimate Vanilla Sugar Cookies (page 13)

2 batches American Buttercream (page 17), divided and dyed in the following amounts:

2 cups (454 g) cinder rose light (page 19)

2 cups (454 g) terracotta (page 22)

2 cups (454 g) pine (page 21)

2 cups (454 g) moss (page 21)

SUPPLIES

Prickly Pears template (page 133)

8 piping bags

4 #32 Wilton piping tips

4 #8B Wilton piping tips

1. Prepare the sugar cookie dough. Cut the dough with the Prickly Pears template (page 133) and bake the cookies. Prepare the buttercream and measure it into small mixing bowls. Color the buttercream according to the Buttercream Color Guide (page 18).

2. Fill four piping bags fitted with a #32 Wilton piping tip and four piping bags fitted with an #8B Wilton piping tip with each color of the buttercream to create an equal amount of cookies in each color. I used the moss buttercream in my example. You can start with that, too, and repeat with the other three colors of buttercream. You will be able to make about five cookies in each color.

3. Starting with the smallest branches of the prickly pear cookie, hold the piping bag at a 90° angle with the tip against the surface of the cookie and begin to apply pressure until you have formed a small dome of buttercream (about the size of the rounded area of the cookie). Then begin to drag the buttercream down the branch of the cookie, reducing the pressure as you end the design. Repeat on the second small branch of the prickly pear.

4. Using the piping bag fitted with a #8B Wilton piping tip in the same color, begin piping the top-most branches on the opposite side of the cactus, repeating the technique in step 3.

5. Repeat these steps as you work your way toward the bottom branches of the cookie. Start with the parts overlapping what you piped, making it slightly larger and following the shape of the cookie.

6. To pipe the flower buds on the top branches, use the piping bag of cinder rose light fit with the #32 Wilton piping tip. Holding the piping bag with the tip against the top edge of the cookie, gently apply pressure until you have formed a small dome of buttercream. Slowly reduce pressure as you pull upward, creating a peak and ending the design.

7. Repeat steps 3 through 6 with the remaining cookies. Refill the piping bags with buttercream as needed. Leftover buttercream can be stored in an airtight container in the fridge for up to 1 week and in the freezer for up to 3 months.

*See beauty photo on page 62.

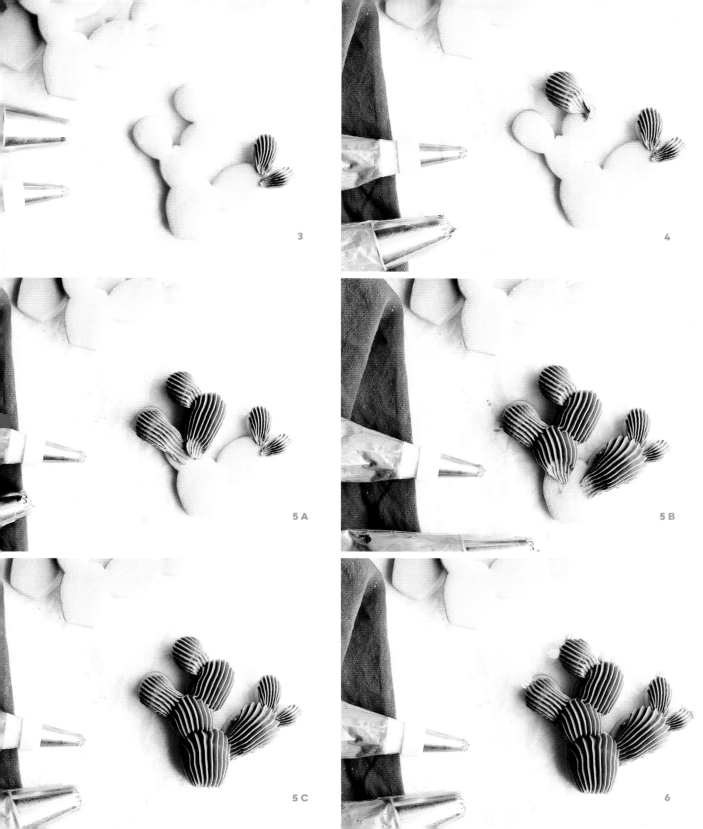

3

4

5 A

5 B

5 C

6

DESERT LIGHTNING BUGS

Lightning bugs remind us of childhood wonder, of dreams. They spark our imagination as they float through the night sky like tiny stars. Fireflies have significant meaning in folklore. They serve as a reminder of "a little light shining bravely in the darkness." At dusk, just as the stars are peeking out, the fireflies make an appearance. They are pure magic as they dance across the foliage with their twinkling lights aglow. These little bugs with their sugar paper wings are a fun reminder that magic does exist in nature.

INGREDIENTS

½ batch Ultimate Vanilla Sugar Cookies (page 13)

½ batch American Buttercream (page 17), divided and dyed in the following amounts:

1 cup (227 g) cerise pink (page 19)

½ cup (114 g) golden carrot (page 20)

½ cup (114 g) swan wing (page 22)

½ cup (114 g) black (page 19)

1 sheet pink wafer paper

SUPPLIES

Desert Lightning Bugs template (page 133)

Bug Wings templates (page 134)

Sharp scissors

4 piping bags

4 #2 Wilton piping tips

Small offset spatula

1. Prepare the sugar cookie dough. Cut the dough with the Desert Lightning Bug template (page 133) and bake the cookies. Prepare the buttercream and measure it into small mixing bowls. Color the buttercream according to the Buttercream Color Guide (page 18).

2. Using the Bug Wings templates (page 134) and sharp scissors, cut out one set of wings per bug from the pink wafer paper. Set aside.

3. Fill a piping bag fitted with a #2 Wilton piping tip with the cerise pink buttercream. Pipe the outline of the bug, starting at the outer edge with the tip of the piping bag parallel to the cookie surface. Gently apply pressure as you slowly lift up, letting the buttercream fall to the surface of the cookie. When you have gone entirely around the outer edge, release pressure to end the line.

4. Using the piping bag of cerise pink fitted with a #2 Wilton piping tip, fill in the head of the bug and one-third of the body. Starting at the tip of the bug's head, gently apply pressure and move in a zig-zag motion as you slowly move toward the bottom of the bug's body.

5. Fill a piping bag fitted with a #2 Wilton piping tip with the golden carrot buttercream. Fill in one-third of the bug's body. Starting just below the head of the bug, with the tip of the piping bag perpendicular to the cookie surface, gently apply pressure and move in a zig-zag motion as you slowly move toward the bottom of the bug's body.

6. Fill a piping bag fitted with a #2 Wilton piping tip with the swan wing buttercream. Fill in the final third of the bug's body. Starting just below the head of the bug, with the tip of the piping bag parallel to the cookie surface, gently apply pressure and move in a zig-zag motion as you slowly move toward the bottom of the bug's body. If you want to create different hues on different cookies, you could also fill in the colors in different layers and orders.

(continued)

7. Using a small offset spatula, smooth out the surface of the bugs (see tips for smoothing buttercream in the Cookie Basics section on page 9).

8. Fill a piping bag fitted with a #2 Wilton piping tip with the black buttercream. To add eyes to the bugs, pipe a small dot of buttercream on the front edge of the bug's head just left of center. Repeat on the other side.

9. Using the piping bag of cerise pink fitted with the number #2 Wilton piping tip, pipe two large dots just below the head of the bug roughly an ⅛ inch (3 mm) apart.

10. Using four of the cut-out Bug Wings per bug, position the top right and bottom right wings together and gently push the tip into the buttercream in the center of the two dots. Spread the wings apart slightly. Repeat this step on the left side. Using the piping bag of cerise pink fitted with a #2 Wilton piping tip, pipe a dot in the center of the wings.

11. Repeat steps 3 through 10 with the remaining cookies. Refill the piping bags with buttercream as needed. Leftover buttercream can be stored in an airtight container in the fridge for up to 1 week and in the freezer for up to 3 months.

GOLDEN WILD FLOWERS

I first saw these delightful little flowers in Colorado. The little blooms were not yet opened, with their pink and green little fronds tucked tight within the petals. Their magnificent color against the patches of green that dotted the desert landscape was truly beautiful.

INGREDIENTS

1 batch Ultimate Vanilla Sugar Cookies (page 13)

½ batch American Buttercream (page 17), divided and dyed in the following amounts:

½ cup (114 g) golden carrot (page 20)

½ cup (114 g) flamingo pink (page 20)

½ cup (114 g) pine (page 21)

SUPPLIES

Golden Wild Flowers template (page 133)

Piping bag

#2 Wilton piping tip

Small offset spatula

#1 Wilton piping tip

2 tipless piping bags

1. Prepare the sugar cookie dough. Cut the dough with the Golden Wild Flowers template (page 133) and bake the cookies. Prepare the buttercream and measure it into small mixing bowls. Color the buttercream according to the Buttercream Color Guide (page 18).

2. Fill a piping bag fitted with a #2 Wilton piping tip with the golden carrot buttercream to outline the flowers. Pipe four hollow triangle shapes, two pointing to the left with a smaller one underneath, and one pointing to the right. Hold the piping bag at a 140° angle with the tip against the surface of the cookie. Begin to apply pressure slowly as you gently lift the tip slightly away from the surface of the cookie, letting the line fall to the cookie surface.

3. When the outlines are finished, fill in the wild flowers with the golden carrot buttercream. Holding the piping bag at a 90° angle, fill in the outline by gently applying pressure to the piping bag and moving in a zig-zag motion.

4. Use a small offset spatula to smooth out the surface of the flowers (see tips for smoothing buttercream in the Cookie Basics section on page 9).

5. Change the tip on the piping bag of golden carrot buttercream from the #2 Wilton piping tip to a #1 Wilton piping tip. The details consist of simple lines; you can add three or four depending on the size of the flower. Starting with the tip of the piping bag against the surface of the cookie, begin to apply pressure slowly as you lift the tip slightly, letting the buttercream fall into place on the surface of the cookie.

(continued)

6. Fill a tipless piping bag with the flamingo pink buttercream to make the pink fronds. Using sharp scissors, cut a tiny amount off the tip and test the line diameter. Adjust the size of the cut until you achieve your desired line width. Hold the piping bag at a 140° angle with the tip against the cookie surface and vertical to the top of the flower. Begin to slowly apply pressure as you lift up slightly, letting the line fall to the surface of the cookie. Gently release pressure when you are ready to end the line. Repeat this step to create three or four lines for each flower. The final step is to top each frond with a tiny dot of buttercream. Do this using the same piping bag of flamingo pink buttercream. Hold the piping bag at a 90° angle, placing the tip of the bag against the cookie surface at the tip of each frond. Slowly apply pressure until you have a dot, then gently release pressure.

7. Fill a tipless piping bag with the pine buttercream to make the leaves. Using sharp scissors, cut a tiny amount off the tip and test the line diameter. Start with the middle stem. Hold the piping bag at a 90° angle with the tip against the surface of the cookie and slowly apply pressure as you lift slightly away from the cookie, allowing the buttercream to fall onto the surface. When the middle stem is complete, create stems for the other flowers that branch off the main stem, using the same pine buttercream. Holding the piping bag at a 140° angle, start at the widest part of the leaf and apply pressure slowly as you create the rounded end. Slowly release pressure as you move toward the stem, tapering off the leaf.

8. Repeat steps 2 through 7 with the remaining cookies. Refill the piping bags with buttercream as needed. Leftover buttercream can be stored in an airtight container in the fridge for up to 1 week and in the freezer for up to 3 months.

SPOOKY FALL COOKIES

Fall is my favorite time of year. The colors of the changing leaves, the crisp, cool air and, of course, Halloween. If you have ever visited the Sugarbombe website, you have likely noticed the Halloween collection and my love of all things spooky. The designs in this chapter are just a few of my favorites. Using some of the techniques in previous chapters, like rosettes, ruffles and stars, you can create Fall Floral Pumpkins (page 77) and beautiful Rustic Fall Leaves (page 91). Spooky Little Ghosts (page 79) are made using the smoothing technique and Gilded Rose Crown Skulls (page 83) will spark the imagination of all your trick or treaters.

FALL FLORAL PUMPKINS

YIELD: 23 (3-INCH [7.5-CM]) COOKIES

Nothing reminds me of fall quite like pumpkins. In recent years, I have loved seeing the range of varieties available; their unusual shapes and colors have been truly inspiring. For this design, I chose my favorite mauve colors. I encourage you to get creative by choosing your favorite fall color, or follow along with this collection.

INGREDIENTS

1 batch Ultimate Vanilla Sugar Cookies (page 13)

1 batch American Buttercream (page 17), divided and dyed in the following amounts:

1½ cups (341 g) mauve dark, divided (page 21)

1½ cups (341 g) mauve light, divided (page 20)

1½ cups (341 g) mauve medium, divided (page 21)

SUPPLIES

Fall Floral Pumpkins templates (page 134)

6 piping bags

1 #27 Wilton piping tip

1 #856 Ateco piping tip

1 #32 Wilton piping tip

1 #825 Ateco piping tip

1 #22 Wilton piping tip

1 #124 Wilton piping tip

1. Prepare the sugar cookie dough. Cut the dough with the Fall Floral Pumpkins templates (page 134) and bake the cookies. Try to split the dough evenly between the three pumpkin shapes. Prepare the buttercream and measure it into small mixing bowls. Color the buttercream according to the Buttercream Color Guide (page 18).

2. Fill a piping bag fitted a #27 Wilton piping tip with half of the mauve dark buttercream to pipe the stems of the pumpkins. Starting at the base of the stem, hold the piping bag at a 90° angle with the tip of the piping bag perpendicular to the surface of the cookie. Gently apply pressure as you move up the stem, following the design of the cookie. Release pressure and pull the piping bag away to end.

3. Fill a piping bag fitted with a #856 Ateco piping tip with half of the mauve light buttercream and place the remaining mauve light buttercream in a piping bag fitted with a #32 Wilton piping tip. Fill a piping bag fitted with a #825 Ateco piping tip with half of the mauve medium buttercream. Place the remaining mauve medium buttercream in a piping bag fitted with a #22 Wilton piping tip. Fill a piping bag fitted with a #124 Wilton piping tip with the remaining half of the mauve dark buttercream.

4. Pipe rosettes with the piping bags fitted with the mauve light #856 Ateco piping tip and the mauve medium #825 Ateco piping tip. To start a rosette, hold the piping bag at a 90° angle with the tip parallel to the cookie surface. Gently apply pressure as you start in the center of the rosette and work your way outward counter-clockwise in a tight spiral. To end the rosette, gently release pressure to create a tail that will taper into the side of the rosette.

(continued)

5. Pipe ruffles with the piping bag fitted with the mauve dark #124 Wilton piping tip. Hold the piping bag at a 45° angle with the tip against the surface of the cookie and the rounded portion of the tip facing up (the thinner edge produces the ruffle effect). Gently apply pressure as you move the piping tip side to side slightly. To end the ruffle, gently release pressure to create a tail that will taper into the side of the rosette.

6. Fill in the remaining open spaces with dots of stars piped with mauve light #32 and mauve medium #22 Wilton piping tips. Hold the piping bag at a 90° angle parallel to the cookie surface. Gently apply pressure on the piping bag until you have a small round ball of buttercream that is the desired size. Release pressure and pull the piping bag away to end.

7. Repeat steps 2 through 6 with the remaining cookies. Refill the piping bags with buttercream as needed. Leftover buttercream can be stored in an airtight container in the fridge for up to 1 week and in the freezer for up to 3 months.

SPOOKY LITTLE GHOSTS

YIELD: 27 (3-INCH [7.5-CM]) COOKIES

These sweet and spooky little party favors are flavored with sweet vanilla buttercream over a toasty almond cookie. They are a perfect pairing with all your Halloween treats and décor. Lay them out on a table and watch people swoon over how cute they are!

INGREDIENTS

1 batch Almond Bliss Sugar Cookies (page 14)

1 batch American Buttercream (page 17), divided and dyed in the following amounts:

2 cups (454 g) swan wing (page 22)

½ cup (114 g) cinder rose light (page 19)

½ cup (114 g) black (page 19)

SUPPLIES

Spooky Little Ghosts template (page 135)

2 piping bags

2 #2 Wilton piping tips

1 #10 Wilton piping tip

Small offset spatula

Glass of warm water

1 tipless piping bag

1 #1 Wilton piping tip

1. Prepare the sugar cookie dough. Cut the dough with the Spooky Little Ghosts template (page 135) and bake the cookies. Prepare the buttercream and measure it into small mixing bowls. Color the buttercream according to the Buttercream Color Guide (page 18).

2. Fill a piping bag fitted with a #2 Wilton piping tip with the swan wing buttercream to pipe the outline of the ghosts. Holding the piping bag perpendicular to the cookie surface and applying continuous, even pressure, start on the outer edge and follow the edge until you have outlined the entire shape of the ghost. Pay attention at the indents at the bottom and take your time when tracing the curves.

3. Using the same piping bag of swan wing buttercream, change to a #10 Wilton piping tip and begin to fill in the cookie using a zig-zag motion.

4. When the cookie is filled in completely, use a small offset spatula to smooth out the buttercream (see tips for smoothing buttercream in the Cookie Basics section on page 9).

5. Fill a piping bag fitted with a #2 Wilton piping tip with the cinder rose light buttercream to pipe the cheeks. Hold the tip of the piping bag at a 90° angle, pushing into the white frosting slightly, and apply a small amount of pressure until you have a dot the size of a pencil eraser.

(continued)

6. Heat the small offset spatula in a glass of warm water. When the spatula is warm to the touch, place it directly onto the cheek until the cinder rose light buttercream melts into the swan wing buttercream. This technique will help maintain the round shape of the cheek.

7. Fill a tipless piping bag with black buttercream to make the eyes and mouth. With sharp scissors, cut a tiny amount off the tip of the bag to create a small hole capable of piping fine lines. Holding the piping bag slightly above the cheek at a 90° angle right against the surface of the cookie, gently apply pressure until you have a small dot that looks proportionate. Repeat for the second eye. Next, to make the "surprised" mouth, position the tip of the piping bag between the two cheeks and gently apply pressure until you have a small oval.

8. To finish off your ghosts, you will change out the tip of your piping bag of swan wing buttercream to a #1 Wilton piping tip. We will now pipe the outline details on the ghost. Start by outlining the entire ghost. Starting in the bottom left corner, place the tip of your piping bag parallel to the cookie surface. Gently apply pressure as you lift slightly up, letting the buttercream fall to the surface of the cookie. Continue until you have piped a line around the entire outer edge of the cookie. As you approach the starting point, gently release pressure, ending your line.

9. Once the outline is completed, the next step will be to create the ruffle or pleating effect. To do this, extend two lines slightly spaced apart from the indentation along the bottom edge of the cookie. Taper the lines as you release pressure, ending halfway up the cookie.

10. Repeat step 9 on the second indentation and finish this step on all of your cookies.

*See beauty photo on page 74.

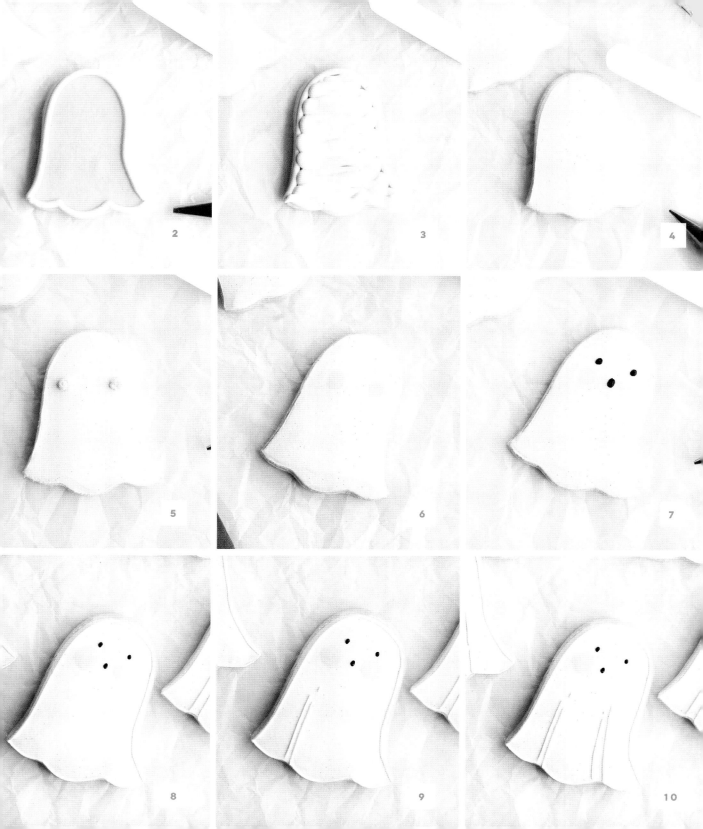

GILDED ROSE CROWN SKULLS

YIELD: 12 (5-INCH [13-CM]) COOKIES

I first created these skulls after a trip to Mexico for the Day of the Dead celebration. The skull represents life and death while the roses are symbolic of beauty and love. The celebration is a beautiful tribute to those loved and lost.

INGREDIENTS

1 batch Ultimate Vanilla Sugar Cookies (page 13)

1 batch American Buttercream (page 17), divided and dyed in the following amounts:

½ cup (114 g) black (page 19)

2 cups (454 g) swan wing (page 22)

1½ cups (341 g) violet light (page 22)

1 cup (227 g) pine (page 21)

SUPPLIES

Gilded Rose Crown Skulls template (page 135)

Food-grade pen

4 piping bags

2 #2 Wilton piping tips

Small offset spatula

Metal scribe

1 #10 Wilton piping tip

1 package 3 x 3–inch (7.5 x 7.5–cm) sheets of food-grade 24K gold

Small paintbrush

1 #124 Wilton piping tip

Parchment paper

1 #366 Wilton piping tip

1. Prepare the sugar cookie dough. Cut the dough with the Gilded Rose Crown Skulls template (page 135) and bake the cookies. Prepare the buttercream and measure it into small mixing bowls. Color the buttercream according to the Buttercream Color Guide (page 18).

2. Cut out the eyes and nose in the Gilded Rose Crown Skulls template. Hold the template over the cookie and trace the eyes and nose onto the cookie with the food-grade pen.

3. Fill a piping bag fitted with a #2 Wilton piping tip with the black buttercream to outline the eyes of the skull. Place the tip of the piping bag perpendicular to the surface of the cookie and gently apply pressure as you lift up slightly, letting the buttercream fall to the surface of the cookie. Repeat for the second eye and the nose.

4. When the outlines are finished, fill in the eyes and nose with the black buttercream. Hold the piping bag perpendicular to the cookie surface starting at the top edge, gently applying pressure as you move in a zig-zag motion.

5. Smooth out the eyes and nose using a small offset spatula (see tips for smoothing buttercream in the Cookie Basics section on page 9). To give the skull a two-dimensional effect, smooth out the buttercream almost to the level of the cookie. Don't worry about going out of the lines; focus more on covering the areas with as little buttercream as possible without letting the cookie show through.

6. Place the Gilded Rose Crown Skulls template back on the cookie. Using a metal scribe, outline the holes of the eyes and nose. Lift the template and make sure you can see the outlines of the eyes and nose in the black buttercream. If the outline is not clearly marked, place the template back on the cookie and outline again.

(continued)

7. Fill a piping bag fitted with a #2 Wilton piping tip with the swan wing buttercream to trace the outlines of the skull. Starting at the outer edge, place the tip of the piping bag perpendicular to the surface of the cookie and gently apply pressure as you lift up slightly, letting the line fall to the surface of the cookie. Outline the entire skull. Using the same technique, outline the eyes and nose following the lines you made with the scribe.

8. Change the #2 Wilton piping tip on the swan wing buttercream to a #10 Wilton piping tip. Holding the tip perpendicular to the surface of the cookie, gently apply pressure until you have filled in the entire surface of the skull except the eyes and nose. I usually do this in big lines or a zig-zag motion.

9. Smooth out the surface of the cookie using the small offset spatula.

10. Again using the piping bag of swan wing buttercream fitted with a #10 tip, pipe the teeth of the skull. Starting in the middle of the cookie, approximately ¼ inch (6 mm) from the bottom, hold the piping bag at a 90° angle against the cookie surface. Gently apply pressure as you move toward the bottom edge. After you pipe each tooth, use the offset spatula to smooth out the tooth by placing the top curved edge of the small offset spatula gently against the top of the tooth and gently pulling downward. Use the edge of the spatula to clean any overhanging buttercream along the bottom edge of the tooth. Repeat for the remaining teeth. I had space for five teeth.

11. Apply the food-grade gold by gently lifting it off the paper with the edge of a paintbrush and placing it on the surface of the skull, approximately ½ inch (13 mm) from the top edge of the eye. Using a paintbrush and very little pressure, smooth the gold onto the buttercream.

12. Fill a piping bag with the violet light buttercream fitted with a #124 Wilton piping tip. Follow the directions for piping roses on page 24. Pipe the roses onto small squares of parchment paper and set them aside to dry for 30 to 60 minutes. When piping roses, make a variety of sizes to ensure a balanced fit to each skull, three to four roses for each skull.

13. When the roses have dried, place a large drop of buttercream on the back of each to attach them to the skull. Arrange the roses on each skull.

14. Fill a piping bag fitted with a #366 Wilton piping tip with the pine buttercream. Pipe leaves to fill in the gaps between the roses. Review how to pipe leaves on page 24.

15. Repeat steps 2 through 14 with the remaining cookies. Refill the piping bags with buttercream as needed. Leftover buttercream can be stored in an airtight container in the fridge for up to 1 week and in the freezer for up to 3 months.

DAY OF THE DEAD CASKET MINIS

YIELD: 14 (4-INCH [10-CM]) COOKIES

If you have visited Sugarbombe in the fall, you will quickly understand how much I adore all of the beautiful and fun celebrations this time of year has to offer. These little minis are no exception, bursting with almond and cinnamon flavor and topped with a single buttercream rosette or as many as you wish. The cookies are a sweet, beautiful reminder of generations past.

INGREDIENTS

1 batch Almond Bliss Sugar Cookies (page 14)

1 tsp cinnamon (optional, see Step 1)

1 batch American Buttercream (page 17), divided and dyed in the following amounts:

1 cup (227 g) black (page 19)

1 cup (227 g) cinder rose light (page 19)

1 cup (227 g) cinder rose medium (page 20)

1 cup (227 g) cinder rose dark (page 20)

½ cup (114 g) pine (page 21)

½ cup (114 g) swan wing (page 22)

SUPPLIES

Day of the Dead Casket Minis template (page 135)

6 piping bags

1 #2 Wilton piping tip

1 #10 Wilton piping tip

Small offset spatula

2 #350 Ateco piping tips

3 #15 Ateco piping tips

2 #1 Wilton piping tips

1. Prepare the sugar cookie dough. If you would like, add 1 teaspoon of cinnamon with the almond flour and whisk to combine before adding the flour. Cut the dough with the Day of the Dead Casket Minis template (page 135) and bake the cookies. Prepare the buttercream and measure it into small mixing bowls. Color the buttercream according to the Buttercream Color Guide (page 18).

2. Fill a piping bag fitted with a #2 Wilton piping tip with black buttercream to outline the casket minis. Starting at a corner of the outer edge of the cookie, hold the piping bag perpendicular to the cookie surface and apply continuous, even pressure. Lift up slightly to let the buttercream fall to the cookie surface. Continue until you have outlined the entire cookie.

3. Change the piping bag of black buttercream with the #2 Wilton piping tip to a #10 Wilton piping tip to fill in the caskets. With the tip of the piping bag perpendicular to the cookie surface, begin at the outer edge of the cookie and, moving in a zig-zag motion, fill in the entire outlined area evenly.

4. When you have filled in all the cookies, use a small offset spatula to smooth out the buttercream (see tips for smoothing buttercream in the Cookie Basics section on page 9).

(continued)

CASKET MINI ONE

5. Fill a piping bag fitted with a #15 Ateco piping tip with the cinder rose light buttercream. Repeat this step for the cinder rose medium and cinder rose dark buttercream to create rosettes. Place the tip of the piping bag of cinder rose light buttercream perpendicular to the cookie surface as you gently apply pressure, making one loop in a counter-clockwise motion from the center of the rosette and ending at the outer edge. Each rosette should be about the size of a pencil eraser. Repeat this step, alternating between cinder rose light, cinder rose medium and cinder rose dark buttercream, until you have covered the surface of the casket, leaving a border of ⅛ to ¼ inch (3–6 mm) around the outside edge.

6. Fill a piping bag fitted with a #350 Ateco piping tip with the pine buttercream to make the leaves between the rosettes. Holding the tip of the piping bag against the surface of the cookie at a 140° angle, apply a small amount of pressure as you slowly lift up, then release pressure to create the tip of the leaf. Add as many or few leaves as you would like. Leaves are a good way to fill in any gaps between rosettes.

7. Fill a piping bag fitted with a #1 Wilton piping tip with the swan wing buttercream to pipe the scalloped edge. Starting at a corner along the edge of the cookie, make a small half-circle, ending parallel to where you started. Repeat this along the entire edge of the cookie.

CASKET MINI TWO

8. Using one of the piping bags filled with cinder rose medium buttercream and fitted with a #15 Ateco piping tip, pipe two rosettes approximately one-third of the way down from the top of the coffin. Place the tip of the piping bag perpendicular to the cookie surface as you gently apply pressure, making one loop in a counter-clockwise motion from the center of the rosette and ending at the outer edge. Repeat this step for the second rosette placed in a slightly staggered but close location to the first.

9. Change the piping bag filled with pine buttercream from the #350 Ateco piping tip to a #1 Wilton piping tip to pipe the stems of the rosettes. Place the tip of the piping bag perpendicular to the surface of the cookie, right under the rosettes. Gently apply pressure, slightly lifting the piping tip and allowing the buttercream to fall into place. Make one thin line, about ½ inch (13 mm) from the bottom of the cookie. Repeat this step for the second stem, crossing it over the first stem.

10. Change the piping bag of pine buttercream from the #1 Wilton piping tip to a #350 Ateco piping tip to create the leaves. Place the tip perpendicular to the stem and slowly apply pressure as you lift up and release pressure. Create one leaf, pointing outward, about midway down the stem. Repeat this step on the second stem.

11. Use the piping bag of swan wing buttercream fitted with a #1 Wilton piping tip to pipe the scallops. Starting at a corner along the edge of the cookie, make a small half-circle, ending parallel to where you started. Repeat this along the entire edge of the cookie.

12. Repeat designs one and two as desired on the remaining cookies. I encourage you to get creative by making a variety of designs with one rosette, two rosettes or many rosettes covering the caskets. Refill the piping bags with buttercream as needed. Leftover buttercream can be stored in an airtight container in the fridge for up to 1 week and in the freezer for up to 3 months.

2

3

4

5 A

5 B

5 C

6

7

8

9

10

11

RUSTIC FALL LEAVES

YIELD: 23 (3-INCH [7.5-CM]) COOKIES

I first made these leaf cookies for a beautiful fall party here in the Pacific Northwest. The request was for a modern take on traditional fall colors. I absolutely loved how the color turned out, so I wanted to share these with you. I encourage you to do the same and feel free to add some of your favorite fall colors.

INGREDIENTS

1 batch Ultimate Vanilla Sugar Cookies (page 13)

½ batch American Buttercream (page 17), dyed in the following amounts:

1 cup (227 g) brick (page 19)

¾ cup (170 g) terracotta (page 22)

¾ cup (170 g) cinder rose light (page 19)

SUPPLIES

Rustic Fall Leaves template (page 134)

3 piping bags

3 #2 Wilton piping tips

3 #124 Wilton piping tips

1. Prepare the sugar cookie dough. Cut the dough with the Rustic Fall Leaves templates (page 134) and bake the cookies. Prepare the buttercream and measure it into small mixing bowls. Color the buttercream according to the Buttercream Color Guide (page 18).

2. Fill a piping bag fitted with a #2 Wilton piping tip with brick buttercream. Starting at the bottom center of the leaf, place the tip of the piping bag against the surface of the cookie and gently apply pressure as you lift up slightly, allowing the buttercream to fall to the cookie surface, creating a line that runs up the middle to the top of the leaf. Release pressure, ending the stem. When the middle stem is complete, create stems that branch off the main one.

3. Change the tip on the piping bag with brick buttercream from a #2 Wilton piping tip to a #124 Wilton piping tip. Place the tip of the piping bag parallel to the cookie surface at a 90° angle, with the thinner part of the tip opening against the outside edge and the wider part of the opening at the stem. Gently apply pressure as you follow the angle of the leaf. When the point of the piping tip reaches the top point of the leaf, repeat this motion to form the opposite side of the leaf.

4. Repeat steps 2 and 3 with the remaining cookies, using the terracotta and cinder rose light buttercream. Refill the piping bags with buttercream as needed. Leftover buttercream can be stored in an airtight container in the fridge for up to 1 week and in the freezer for up to 3 months.

2

3A   3B   3C

WINTER WONDERLAND

Winter is the official season for baking. Growing up in North Dakota, where winter starts in October and ends in May, there were plenty of snow days to bake and create warm memories with food. It has become tradition in my home over the years to create beautiful and delicious cookie platters for neighbors, friends and family as a way to celebrate friendships and show appreciation for those you love and those who support you throughout the year. Using some basic household ingredients and a little creativity, you can create snowmen (page 99) that look like they are covered in fresh snow, magical snowflakes (page 95), candy canes flavored with peppermint (page 111) and sugar-coated gum drops (page 108). These sweet and delightful cookies will surely help to spread holiday cheer to you and yours.

SPARKLING SNOWFLAKES

YIELD: 22 (3½-INCH [9-CM]) COOKIES

Pink snowflakes are the stuff that young girls dream of, and I was no exception. These lightly sweetened pink gems are flavored with peppermint and vanilla, bringing back all the memories of long snow-filled winters and the flavors of the holiday season.

INGREDIENTS

1 batch Ultimate Vanilla Sugar Cookies (page 13)

½ batch American Buttercream (page 17), dyed in the following amount:

2½ cups (568 g) swan wing (page 22)

2 cups (240 g) powdered sugar

3 tbsp (45 ml) water

¼ tsp peppermint extract

Pink food gel coloring

SUPPLIES

Sparkling Snowflakes templates (page 135)

Parchment paper

Sheet pan

Cooling rack

1 piping bag

1 #1 Wilton piping tip

1 #2 Wilton piping tip

1. Prepare the sugar cookie dough. Cut the dough with the Sparkling Snowflakes templates (page 135) and bake the cookies. Prepare the buttercream and measure it into a small mixing bowl. Color the buttercream according to the Buttercream Color Guide (page 18).

2. Place a sheet of parchment paper in a sheet pan and place a cooling rack on the parchment paper. In a medium-sized bowl, mix the powdered sugar, water and peppermint extract until smooth. Add one small drop of pink food gel and mix until the color is consistent throughout. Continue to the next steps and use immediately, as the glaze will form a skin as it begins to dry.

3. Dip the top of a cookie into the glaze. Turn the cookie over and place it on the cooling rack to allow the glaze to dry. Repeat this step with six or seven more cookies.

4. Add an additional drop of pink food gel to the glaze and mix until the color is consistent throughout. It should be slightly pinker than the previous step. Dip the tops of half of the remaining cookies into the glaze and place them on the cooling rack to dry.

5. Add an additional drop of pink food gel to the glaze and mix until the color is consistent throughout and slightly pinker than in step 4. Dip the tops of the remaining cookies into the glaze and place them on the cooling rack to dry.

(continued)

6. When the glaze has dried on all the cookies, fill a piping bag fitted with a #1 Wilton piping tip with half of the swan wing buttercream. Placing the tip of the piping bag parallel to the surface of the cookie, gently apply pressure as you lift up slightly, allowing the buttercream to fall to the cookie surface. Starting at the tip of one of the snowflake's points, pipe a line to the point directly opposite. Repeat until all points are connected and you have three lines.

7. Create a second set of lines that connect the inner points of the snowflake. Place the tip of the piping bag parallel to the surface of the cookie and gently apply pressure as you lift up slightly, allowing the buttercream to fall to the cookie surface. Starting at one indent of the snowflake, pipe a line to the indent directly opposite. Repeat until all the indents are connected and you have another three lines.

8. Working again with the first lines you created, pipe two V-shaped lines off the line in one of the points. Starting at an outer edge of the point, place the tip of the piping bag parallel to the surface of the cookie. Gently apply pressure as you lift up slightly, allowing the buttercream to fall to the cookie surface as you move downward to the line and back up to the opposite outer edge of the point. Repeat on the remaining five points of the snowflake.

9. Working in the inner section of the snowflake, create one V-shaped line on the top portion of one of the lines. Starting at the outer edge of the line, place the tip of the piping bag perpendicular to the surface of the cookie. Gently apply pressure as you lift up slightly, allowing the buttercream to fall to the cookie surface as you move downward to the line and back up to complete the V shape. Repeat on the remaining five inner lines.

10. Change the tip on the piping bag with the swan white buttercream from a #1 Wilton piping tip to a #2 Wilton piping tip. Add a dot of buttercream to the tip of each point of the snowflake, in the middle of the snowflake where the lines adjoin, and at the end of each line in the indents of the snowflake. You will make a total of thirteen dots.

11. Repeat steps 6 through 10 with the remaining cookies. Refill the piping bag with buttercream as needed. Leftover buttercream can be stored in an airtight container in the fridge for up to 1 week and in the freezer for up to 3 months.

2

3

5

6

7

8

9 A

9 B

10

FROSTY SNOWMEN

YIELD: 16 (5¼-INCH [13.5-CM]) COOKIES

These snowmen are sprinkled with coconut and filled with fluffy buttercream. They are sweet little reminders of all the fun-filled snow days from childhood and the memories we made with those near and dear. I hope making these cute snowmen will usher in some new fun memories for you, too.

INGREDIENTS

1 batch Ultimate Vanilla Sugar Cookies (page 13)

2 batches American Buttercream (page 17), divided and dyed in the following amounts:

3 cups (681 g) swan wing (page 22)

1 cup (227 g) ruby (page 22)

1 cup (227 g) pine (page 21)

1 cup (227 g) flamingo pink (page 20)

1 cup (227 g) golden carrot (page 20)

½ cup (114 g) caramel (page 19)

½ cup (114 g) black (page 19)

½ cup (114 g) tiger lily (page 22)

2 cups (186 g) shredded coconut

½ cup (60 g) powdered sugar

SUPPLIES

Frosty Snowmen template (page 136)

8 piping bags

5 #5 Wilton piping tips

Small offset spatula

4 #45 Wilton piping tips

3 #1 Wilton piping tips

1 #2 Wilton piping tip

1. Prepare the sugar cookie dough. Cut the dough with the Frosty Snowmen template (page 136) and bake the cookies. Prepare the buttercream and measure it into small mixing bowls. Color the buttercream according to the Buttercream Color Guide (page 18).

2. Add the shredded coconut and the powdered sugar to a food processor. Pulse four to five times for 1 to 2 seconds each pulse to achieve a "snowy" texture. Place in a medium bowl and set aside.

3. Fill a piping bag fitted with a #5 Wilton piping tip with the swan wing buttercream to outline the face and the body of the snowman, omitting the area for the scarf and hat. Starting at the left or right curve of the head, hold the tip of the piping bag parallel to the surface of the cookie. Gently apply pressure as you lift slightly upward, allowing the line of buttercream to fall to the cookie surface. Pipe the two rounded edges of the snowman's head, and straight lines to outline the hat and scarf. Repeat this step to outline the body of the snowman, leaving a straight line to indicate the bottom of the scarf.

4. Using the same piping bag of swan wing buttercream, fill in the face and body. Holding the tip of the piping bag parallel to the cookie surface, gently apply pressure as you move in a zig-zag motion, filling in the outlined areas completely.

5. Repeat steps 3 and 4 with all the cookies. Use a small offset spatula to smooth out the buttercream (see tips for smoothing buttercream in the Cookie Basics section on page 9).

6. Sprinkle the shredded coconut mixture over the cookie. Do not press the cookie into the coconut or it will create a flat surface and cause the buttercream to spread over the edges. Repeat steps 5 and 6 with all the cookies.

(continued)

7. Fill four piping bags fitted with #45 Wilton piping tips with the ruby, pine, flamingo pink and golden carrot buttercream. Choose one of the colors and begin piping a scarf. Holding the tip of the piping bag at a 140° angle with the widest side parallel to the cookie surface, apply pressure as you fill in the area between the head and the body to create a scarf.

8. Starting at the top right edge of the scarf, hold the tip of the piping bag with the widest side parallel to the cookie surface. Gently apply pressure as you continue down the scarf's tail to the longest point. Repeat this step for the shorter tail, ending at the notch just above the previous scarf tail. Continue piping scarves with the remaining three colors, making as many of each color as you would like.

9. Change the tip of the piping bag with the color you piped the scarf with from a #45 Wilton piping tip to a #5 Wilton piping tip. Using the same four corresponding colors you created the scarves with, outline, fill in and smooth out the hat of the snowman. Using the piping bag of swan wing buttercream fitted with a #5 Wilton piping tip, pipe a dot to create the pom-pom at the end of the hat.

10. Fill two piping bags fitted with #1 Wilton piping tips with the caramel and black buttercream. Fill a third piping bag fitted with a #2 Wilton piping tip with tiger lily buttercream.

11. Starting with the piping bag of black buttercream, pipe three dots down the center of the snowman body for his buttons. Use the same piping bag to pipe two dots for eyes. To make the smile, pipe a row of dots, starting slightly below and to the left of the snowman's left eye. Continue to pipe dots in the shape of a smile, ending slightly lower and to the right of the opposite eye.

12. Using the tiger lily buttercream, pipe the carrot nose. Holding the tip at a 90° angle against the surface of the cookie, slowly apply pressure as you lift up and slightly back down to create a wider, more irregular carrot-like shape. Slowly ease off the pressure as you continue to lift upward, creating the point of the carrot.

13. Use the caramel buttercream to pipe the snowman's arms. Starting on the bottom right edge of the scarf with the tip of the piping bag against the surface of the cookie, slowly apply pressure as you lift slightly upward, allowing the buttercream to fall into place as you create a stick-like arm. Repeat on the left side.

14. Change the piping bag of swan wing buttercream from a #5 Wilton piping tip to a #1 Wilton piping tip to create designs on the scarf and hat. These can be as simple as dots or lines, or a more complicated snowflake pattern.

15. Repeat steps 7 through 14 with the remaining cookies. Refill the piping bags with buttercream as needed. Leftover buttercream can be stored in an airtight container in the fridge for up to 1 week and in the freezer for up to 3 months.

FANCIFUL HOLIDAY TREES

It wouldn't be Christmas without a holiday tree. Covered in billowy buttercream and topped off with your favorite sprinkles, these are sure to be a favorite. This is a very beginner-friendly design, and you will love the way the sprinkles capture the twinkling lights.

INGREDIENTS

1 batch Ultimate Vanilla Sugar Cookies (page 13)

1 batch American Buttercream (page 17), divided and dyed in the following amounts:

2½ cups (568 g) pine (page 21)

2½ cups (568 g) green tea (page 20)

Assorted sprinkles

SUPPLIES

Fanciful Holiday Trees templates (pages 136–137)

2 piping bags

2 #865 Ateco piping tips

1. Prepare the sugar cookie dough. Cut the dough with the Fanciful Holiday Trees templates (pages 136–137) and bake the cookies. Prepare the buttercream and measure it into small mixing bowls. Color the buttercream according to the Buttercream Color Guide (page 18).

2. Fill a piping bag fitted with a #865 Ateco piping tip with the pine buttercream, and the other piping bag fitted with a #865 Ateco piping tip with the green tea buttercream.

3. Starting with either shade of green, at the outer tip of the lowest left branch, place the tip of the piping bag perpendicular to the surface of the cookie at a 90° angle. Gently apply pressure as you slowly rotate to a 45° angle, moving upward toward the next set of branches. Repeat this step, creating five to six branches along the bottom tier of the tree.

4. Repeating step 3, continue to the next tier of branches, creating one fewer branch per tier. For the taller cookies, you can create three to four tiers. For the shorter cookies, you can create two tiers.

5. Add your favorite sprinkles.

6. Repeat steps 3 to 5 with the other shade of green, splitting the cookies evenly between the two shades. Refill the piping bags with buttercream as needed. Leftover buttercream can be stored in an airtight container in the fridge for up to 1 week and in the freezer for up to 3 months.

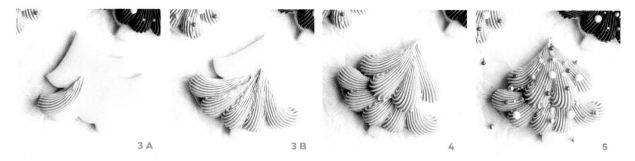

3 A   3 B   4   5

GINGERBREAD MEN

The gingerbread man is said to date back as far as Queen Elizabeth I of England, who presented visiting dignitaries with gingerbread men baked in their likeness. Later they were tied with ribbons and given as symbols of love and eventually they became part of a children's story. The holidays are always about those near to our hearts, so what could be better than giving these sweet little guys to those we love?

INGREDIENTS

1 batch Ultimate Vanilla Sugar Cookies (page 13)

1 batch American Buttercream (page 17), divided and dyed in the following amounts:

2 cups (454 g) caramel (page 19)

½ cup (114 g) flamingo pink (page 20)

½ cup (114 g) black (page 19)

½ cup (114 g) golden carrot (page 20)

½ cup (114 g) green tea (page 20)

½ cup (114 g) swan wing (page 22)

SUPPLIES

Gingerbread Men template (page 137)

6 piping bags

1 #5 Wilton piping tip

Small offset spatula

5 #2 Wilton piping tips

1 #1 Wilton piping tip

1. Prepare the sugar cookie dough. Cut the dough with the Gingerbread Men template (page 137) and bake the cookies. Prepare the buttercream and measure it into small mixing bowls. Color the buttercream according to the Buttercream Color Guide (page 18).

2. Fill a piping bag fitted with a #5 Wilton piping tip with the caramel buttercream to outline the gingerbread man. Starting at the outer edge of the head, hold the tip of the piping bag perpendicular to the surface of the cookie. Gently apply pressure as you lift slightly upward, allowing the line of buttercream to fall to the cookie surface. Continue until the entire cookie is outlined.

3. Using the same piping bag of caramel buttercream, fill in the gingerbread man. Holding the tip of the piping bag perpendicular to the cookie surface, gently apply pressure as you move in a zig-zag motion, filling in the outlined areas completely.

4. Repeat steps 2 and 3 with all the cookies. Then, use a small offset spatula to smooth out the buttercream (see tips for smoothing buttercream in the Cookie Basics section on page 9). When smoothing the buttercream, you can add depth by creating a slightly rounded surface in the center.

5. Fill a piping bag fitted with a #2 Wilton piping tip with flamingo pink and pipe two large dots for cheeks. Using the small offset spatula, smooth out the cheeks.

(continued)

6. Fill a piping bag fitted with a #2 Wilton piping tip with black buttercream and pipe two dots for eyes. Change the tip on the piping bag of caramel buttercream from a #5 Wilton piping tip to a #2 Wilton piping tip and pipe a small dot for a nose.

7. Fit two piping bags with #2 Wilton piping tips and fill one with golden carrot buttercream and the second with green tea buttercream. Pipe out a dot of each color to make two buttons and one on the top of each foot. Using the flamingo pink buttercream piping bag fitted with a #2 Wilton piping tip, pipe out another dot to make a third button.

8. Fill a piping bag fitted with a #1 Wilton piping tip with swan wing buttercream to add the swirls to the hands, feet and top of the head. Place the tip of the piping bag perpendicular to the lower edge of the left arm. Gently apply pressure as you lift up slightly, allowing the buttercream to fall to the cookie surface as you move upward and slightly right. Allow the buttercream to loop over itself and end at the top of the left arm, across from where you started. Repeat this step on the remaining hands, feet and the top of the head.

9. Using the swan wing buttercream piping bag fitted with a #1 Wilton piping tip, make a bow. First, pipe a line that slightly curves downward across the neckline. Second, pipe two extended loops, one off to the left and the second to the right. Then, pipe the tails of the bow. Starting with the tip of the piping bag at the top-left corner at the base of the head and perpendicular to the cookie surface, gently apply pressure as you lift up slightly, allowing the buttercream to fall to the cookie surface. End at the same point on the opposite side. You can give the line a slight curve to create a more natural-looking bow.

10. Repeat steps 4 through 9 with the remaining cookies. Refill the piping bags with buttercream as needed. Leftover buttercream can be stored in an airtight container in the fridge for up to 1 week and in the freezer for up to 3 months.

GUM DROPS

YIELD: 37 (1-INCH [2.5-CM]) COOKIES

These little dreams are a simple design that's easy to pipe. I usually like to pair them with my Gingerbread Men (page 104) at holiday parties.

INGREDIENTS

1 batch Ultimate Vanilla Sugar Cookies (page 13)

½ batch American Buttercream (page 17), divided and dyed in the following amounts:

¾ cup (171 g) apple (page 18)

¾ cup (171 g) golden carrot (page 20)

¾ cup (171 g) flamingo pink (page 20)

1 cup (192 g) sanding sugar

SUPPLIES

Gum Drops template (page 136)

3 piping bags

3 #2 Wilton piping tips

Small offset spatula

1. Prepare the sugar cookie dough. Cut the dough with the Gum Drops template (page 136) and bake the cookies. Prepare the buttercream and measure it into small mixing bowls. Color the buttercream according to the Buttercream Color Guide (page 18).

2. Fit three piping bags with #2 Wilton piping tips. Fill one with apple buttercream, one with golden carrot buttercream and one with flamingo pink buttercream.

3. Choose one of the three colors. Begin icing the gum drops by outlining the outer edge. Hold the tip of the piping bag perpendicular to the surface of the cookie. Gently apply pressure as you lift slightly upward, allowing the line of buttercream to fall to the cookie surface. Release pressure when the outline is complete.

4. Using the same color you used in step 3, fill in the outline. Starting at the top of the gum drop with the tip of the piping bag perpendicular to the cookie surface, gently apply pressure as you move in a zig-zag motion. Continue in this manner until the outline is filled in.

5. Using a small offset spatula, smooth out the surface of the gum drops (see tips for smoothing buttercream in the Cookie Basics section on page 9).

6. Sprinkle the gum drop with the sanding sugar. Do not press the cookie into the sanding sugar because it will spread the buttercream over the edges.

7. Repeat steps 3 through 6 with the remaining cookies, dividing the three colors up evenly among the cookies. Refill the piping bags with buttercream as needed. Leftover buttercream can be stored in an airtight container in the fridge for up to 1 week and in the freezer for up to 3 months.

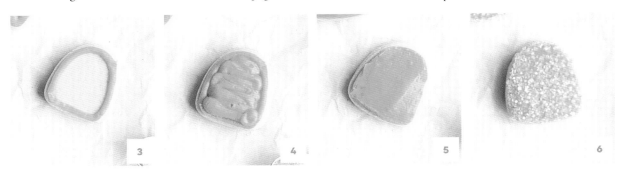

3   4   5   6

FESTIVE CANDY CANES

Candy canes are one of the original holiday candies. Beautiful on their own, mixed into a cookie platter or dipped in hot cocoa, these are sure to be a hit!

INGREDIENTS

1 batch Ultimate Vanilla Sugar Cookies (page 13)

½ batch American Buttercream (page 17), divided and dyed in the following amounts:

½ cup (114 g) ruby (page 22)

½ cup (114 g) cerise pink (page 19)

½ cup (114 g) pine (page 21)

½ cup (114 g) golden carrot (page 20)

2 cups (240 g) powdered sugar

3 tbsp (45 ml) water

Pink food gel

SUPPLIES

Festive Candy Canes template (page 137)

Parchment paper

Sheet pan

Cooling rack

4 piping bags

4 #1 Wilton piping tips

1 #2 Wilton piping tip

1. Prepare the sugar cookie dough. Cut the dough with the Festive Candy Canes template (page 137) and bake the cookies. Prepare the buttercream and measure it into small mixing bowls. Color the buttercream according to the Buttercream Color Guide (page 18).

2. Place a sheet of parchment paper in a sheet pan and place a cooling rack on the parchment paper. In a medium-sized bowl, mix the powdered sugar and water until smooth. Add one drop of pink food gel and mix until the color is a consistent light pink throughout. Use immediately, as the glaze will form a skin as it begins to dry.

3. Dip the top of a cookie into the glaze. Turn the cookie over and place it on the cooling rack to allow the glaze to dry. Continue with the rest of the cookies.

4. Fill a piping bag fitted with a #1 Wilton piping tip with the ruby buttercream. Fill a second bag fitted with a #1 Wilton piping tip with the cerise pink. Using the ruby buttercream, place the tip of the piping bag parallel to the surface of the cookie and slowly apply pressure as you lift up slightly, allowing the buttercream to fall as you make a diagonal line across the candy cane. Repeat with the cerise pink slightly above the ruby line. Continue with this pattern until the entire candy cane is covered.

(continued)

5. Fill a piping bag fitted with a #1 Wilton piping tip with pine buttercream. Starting at the tip of the left leaf, place the tip of the piping bag parallel to the cookie surface. Gently apply pressure as you lift up slightly, allowing the buttercream to fall to the cookie surface, ending the line roughly halfway up the candy cane. Repeat on the opposite side.

6. Using the same piping bag of pine buttercream, pipe the needles onto the stem by placing the tip of the piping bag on the top of the center line. Gently apply pressure as you lift slightly up, allowing the buttercream to fall to the cookie surface, moving in a diagonal line and releasing pressure once you reach the edge. Repeat until the entire stem is filled in on both sides, creating the lines very close together and slightly on top of each other.

7. Change the tip of the ruby buttercream from a #1 Wilton piping tip to a #2 Wilton piping tip to pipe the bow on top of the greenery. With the tip of the piping bag positioned in the center and at the top of the greenery, against the cookie surface, gently apply pressure and lift up slightly as you create a loop, ending in the same position you started. Repeat on the opposite side. Review my tips for creating loops on page 23.

8. With the same piping bag of ruby buttercream, pipe the ribbon strands. With the tip of the piping bag perpendicular to the cookie surface where the two loops meet, begin to apply pressure as you lift up slightly, allowing the buttercream to fall to the surface of the cookie, creating the tail of the bow. Trail the ribbon strands down the branches. Repeat on the opposite side.

9. Fill a piping bag fitted with a #1 Wilton piping tip with the golden carrot buttercream. Holding the piping bag at a 90° angle against the cookie surface, begin to apply pressure to create small dots that resemble berries on the branches. Repeat on the opposite side.

10. Repeat steps 4 through 9 with the remaining cookies. Refill the piping bags with buttercream as needed. Leftover buttercream can be stored in an airtight container in the fridge for up to 1 week and in the freezer for up to 3 months.

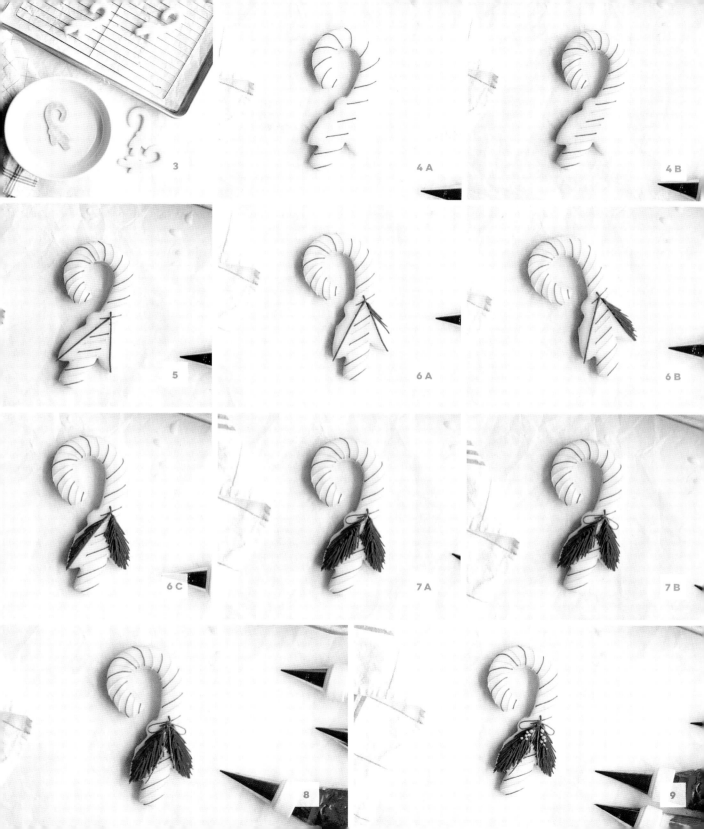

WILD WOODLAND

Living in the Pacific Northwest for the past 25 years has taught me the beauty of the outdoors and the signs of home—the natural wild flowers, the pinecones that come in every shape and size and the mushrooms that are everywhere. Whenever I am planning an event, baking for fun or planning my holiday cookie boxes, these magical little symbols of home are always included. In this chapter, you will use flower tips to create pinecones (page 126) and wild daisies (page 117) and a layered smoothing technique with lines to create mushrooms (page 122) that even the most discerning gnome wouldn't pass up.

WILD WOODLAND DAISIES

YIELD: 16 (3-INCH [7.5-CM]) COOKIES

Daisies may not be the most fragrant or beautiful, but they are a happy little flower. I oftentimes add them to spring bouquets, but they also find their way into the details on fall cookies, and sometimes you may even find a little Santa with one tucked into his hat. If you like daisies as much as I do, be sure to check out the Dainty Daisies cookies on page 47. I made this cookie in white for a classic look, but you could easily swap in one of my pink buttercream hues.

INGREDIENTS

1 batch Ultimate Vanilla Sugar Cookies (page 13)

½ batch American Buttercream (page 17), divided and dyed in the following amounts:

¾ cup (170 g) pine (page 21)

1 cup (227 g) swan wing (page 22)

¾ cup (170 g) golden carrot (page 20)

SUPPLIES

Wild Woodland Daisies template (page 137)

3 piping bags

2 #2 Wilton piping tips

Small offset spatula

1 #124 Wilton piping tip

1. Prepare the sugar cookie dough. Cut the dough with the Wild Woodland Daisies template (page 137) and bake the cookies. Prepare the buttercream and measure it into small mixing bowls. Color the buttercream according to the Buttercream Color Guide (page 18).

2. Fill a piping bag fitted with a #2 Wilton piping tip with the pine buttercream for the leaves of the daisy. Place the tip of the piping bag perpendicular to the cookie surface and, starting on the lower edge in the middle of the two leaves, move up to the point of the right leaf and then back to the center. Repeat this for the left leaf.

3. Using the same piping bag of pine fitted with a #2 Wilton piping tip, fill in the leaves. Start at the tip of the leaf and move toward the bottom in a zig-zag motion.

4. Using a small offset spatula, smooth out the surface of the leaves (see tips for smoothing buttercream in the Cookie Basics section on page 9).

5. Using the piping bag of pine buttercream fitted with a #2 Wilton piping tip, pipe the stem. Place the tip of the piping bag against the surface of the cookie at the center point where the two leaves adjoin. Gently apply pressure as you lift up slightly, allowing the buttercream to fall to the cookie surface. Release pressure, ending the stem a third of the way down from the top of the cookie.

(continued)

6. Fill a piping bag fitted with a #124 Wilton piping tip with the swan wing buttercream to make the petals. Holding the wider end of the petal tip closest to you with the thin end at the top of the petal at a 180° angle against the cookie surface, apply pressure to create the wider part of the petal and gently let up on the pressure as you drag the tip toward the center of the cookie. Repeat this step for each petal.

7. Fill a piping bag fitted with a #2 Wilton piping tip with the golden carrot buttercream to create the center of the daisy. Starting in the center of the cookie with the tip of the piping bag perpendicular to the cookie surface, begin to apply pressure as you gently lift up, allowing the buttercream to fall to the cookie surface, creating the outline for the center.

8. Using the same piping bag of golden carrot buttercream, fill in the outline. Starting in the center of the outline, gently apply pressure as you move the tip in a circular motion until you have reached the outer edge.

9. Using the small offset spatula, smooth out the center of the daisy.

10. Begin the center detail using the same piping bag of golden carrot buttercream. Holding the tip against the outer edge of the center of the daisy, begin to slowly apply pressure until you have created a small dot, then gently release pressure and lift up and away to finish the dot. Repeat this step, working from the outer edge inward, until you have covered the entire center with dots.

11. Repeat steps 2 through 10 with the remaining cookies. Refill the piping bags with buttercream as needed. Leftover buttercream can be stored in an airtight container in the fridge for up to 1 week and in the freezer for up to 3 months.

2

4

5

5 B

7

MAGIC LITTLE ACORNS

Acorns are seen as symbols of good luck, abundance, wisdom and youth—just to name a few. For me they are a symbol of home, a reminder of many long walks in the woods. A box of acorn cookies given to a friend or new neighbor can be a very sweet and meaningful gift.

INGREDIENTS

1 batch Ultimate Vanilla Sugar Cookies (page 13)

1 batch American Buttercream (page 17), divided and dyed in the following amounts:

3 cups (681 g) mocha, divided (page 21)

1 cup (227 g) pine (page 21)

SUPPLIES

Magical Little Acorns template (page 138)

3 piping bags

1 #2 Wilton piping tip

Small offset spatula

1 #352 Wilton piping tip

1 #366 Wilton piping tip

1. Prepare the sugar cookie dough. Cut the dough with the Magic Little Acorns template (page 138) and bake the cookies. Prepare the buttercream and measure it into small mixing bowls. Color the buttercream according to the Buttercream Color Guide (page 18).

2. Fill a piping bag fitted with a #2 Wilton piping tip with 1½ cups (341 g) of the mocha buttercream to create the outline of the stem and bottom portion of the acorn. Starting at the outer edge with the tip of the piping bag perpendicular to the cookie surface, gently apply pressure as you slowly lift up, letting the buttercream fall to the surface. When you have gone all the way around the outer edge of the bottom portion, release pressure to end the line. Repeat this step to outline the stem of the acorn.

3. Using the same bag of mocha buttercream, fill in the two areas. Starting at the top of the stem, gently apply pressure as you move in a zig-zag motion, creating lines to fill the outline of the stem completely. Repeat this step for the lower portion of the acorn.

4. Using a small offset spatula, smooth out the stem and lower body of the acorn (see tips for smoothing buttercream in the Cookie Basics section on page 9).

5. Fill a piping bag fitted with a #352 Wilton piping tip with 1½ cups (341 g) of the mocha buttercream. Starting along the top edge of the lower body of the acorn, hold the piping bag at a 45° angle with the open sides of the tip perpendicular to the cookie surface. Gently apply pressure to create the body of the leaf shape. When you have the desired shape and size, ease off the pressure as you move in a downward motion to create the tip of the leaf. Repeat this motion until you have covered the cap of the acorn with leaves.

6. Repeat step 5 with the other cookies.

7. Fill a piping bag fitted with a #366 Wilton piping tip with the pine buttercream. Starting in the area where the stem meets the body of the acorn, hold the piping bag at a 45° angle with the open sides of the tip parallel to the surface of the cookie. Gently apply pressure to create the body of the leaf shape. When you have the desired shape and size, release pressure as you move in a downward motion to create the tip of the leaf. Repeat this step to create a second leaf.

8. Repeat steps 2 through 7 with the remaining cookies. Refill the piping bags with buttercream as needed. Leftover buttercream can be stored in an airtight container in the fridge for up to 1 week and in the freezer for up to 3 months.

*See beauty image on page 114.

MYTHICAL MUSHROOMS

Mushrooms are those magical little fungi in children's books that make little homes for mice, gnomes and other sweet forest creatures. We use warm colors in this project to capture their earthy tones, but with a bit of imaginative spark. Friends, loved ones and fans of magical stories will feel honored receiving a batch of these little beauties.

INGREDIENTS

1 batch Ultimate Vanilla Sugar Cookies (page 13)

1½ batches American Buttercream (page 17), divided and dyed in the following amounts:

1½ cups (341 g) swan wing, divided (page 22)

1½ cups (341 g) ruby (page 22)

1½ cups (341 g) apple (page 18)

1½ cups (341 g) caramel (page 19)

SUPPLIES

Mythical Mushrooms template (page 138)

5 piping bags

4 #2 Wilton piping tips

Small offset spatula

1 #1 Wilton piping tip

1 # 126K Ateco piping tip

1. Prepare the sugar cookie dough. Cut the dough with the Mythical Mushrooms template (page 138) and bake the cookies. Prepare the buttercream and measure it into small mixing bowls. Color the buttercream according to the Buttercream Color Guide (page 18).

2. Fill a piping bag fitted with a #2 Wilton piping tip with ¾ cup (170 g) of the swan wing buttercream to create the outline of the stem and bottom portion of the mushroom. Starting at the outer edge with the tip of the piping bag perpendicular to the cookie surface, gently apply pressure as you slowly lift up, letting the buttercream fall to the surface of the cookie. When you have gone around the outer edge of the stem, release pressure to end the line.

3. When you have the outline complete, fill in the stem. Starting at the top of the stem, gently apply pressure as you move in a zig-zag motion, creating lines to fill the outline of the stem and the bottom portion of the mushroom completely.

4. Using a small offset spatula, smooth out the stem and lower body of the mushroom (see tips for smoothing buttercream in the Cookie Basics section on page 9).

5. Change the tip on the piping bag of swan wing buttercream from a #2 Wilton to a #1 Wilton piping tip. Starting at the center of the bottom portion of the mushroom cap, place the tip of the piping bag perpendicular to the cookie surface. Gently apply pressure as you slowly lift up, letting the buttercream fall to the surface of the cookie, making short thin lines that angle slightly toward the edge of the mushroom cap.

(continued)

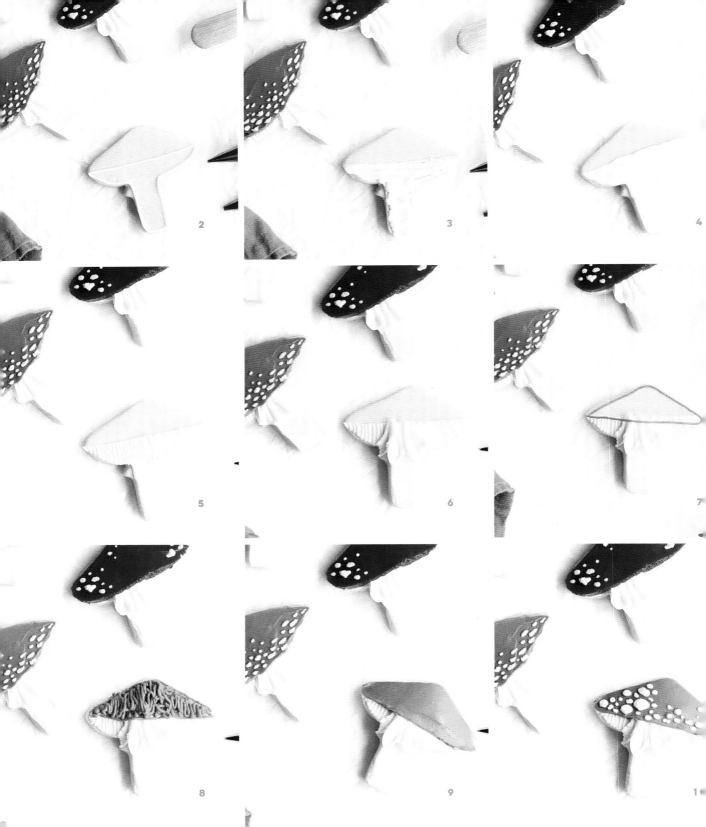

6. Fill a new piping bag fitted with a #126K Ateco piping tip with the remaining ¾ cup (170 g) of the swan wing buttercream. Holding the piping bag at a 45° angle with the curved edge of the piping tip pointed toward the base of the mushroom stem (the narrow edge of the piping tip produces the ruffles), apply even pressure on the piping bag as you move the tip across the fluted area just under the mushroom cap.

7. Choose ruby, apple or caramel for the mushroom cap. Fill a piping bag fitted with a #2 Wilton piping tip with the color you chose. Starting at the outer edge of the cap, place the piping tip perpendicular to the cookie surface and gently apply pressure as you lift up slightly, allowing the line to fall to the cookie surface. Continue until the cap has been completely outlined.

8. Using the same piping bag and color, fill the mushroom cap. Starting at the edge, gently apply pressure as you move in a zig-zag motion, filling in the cap completely.

9. Using the small offset spatula, smooth out the surface of the mushroom cap.

10. Use the piping bag of swan wing buttercream fitted with either a #2 or #1 Wilton piping tip to make spots on the mushroom cap. Place the tip of the piping bag perpendicular to the cookie surface and gently apply pressure until the desired size of the dot is formed. Repeat this step for the desired number of dots.

11. Repeat steps 2 through 10 with the remaining cookies, dividing them equally between the remaining two buttercream colors. Refill the piping bags with buttercream as needed. Leftover buttercream can be stored in an airtight container in the fridge for up to 1 week and in the freezer for up to 3 months.

PINECONE BOUQUET

YIELD: 16 (4-INCH [10-CM]) COOKIES

Pinecones have been an essential part of my love of all things woodland. They make their way into every holiday and tablescape, never stealing the spotlight but always adding an element of whimsy and nostalgia. I like to pair these cookies with my Sparkling Snowflakes (page 95) around the holidays.

INGREDIENTS

1 batch Ultimate Vanilla Sugar Cookies (page 13)

1 batch American Buttercream (page 17), divided and dyed in the following amounts:

1 cup (227 g) cerise pink (page 19)

½ cup (114 g) pine (page 21)

3 cups (681 g) mocha (page 21)

½ cup (114 g) ruby (page 22)

SUPPLIES

Pinecone Bouquet template (page 138)

4 piping bags

1 #2 Wilton piping tip

Small offset spatula

2 #1 Wilton piping tips

2 #5 Wilton piping tips

1 #81 Wilton piping tip

1. Prepare the sugar cookie dough. Cut the dough with the Pinecone Bouquet template (page 138) and bake the cookies. Prepare the buttercream and measure it into small mixing bowls. Color the buttercream according to the Buttercream Color Guide (page 18).

2. Fill a piping bag fitted with a #2 Wilton piping tip with cerise pink buttercream to outline and fill in the cookie. Holding the piping bag perpendicular to the cookie surface and applying continuous, even pressure, start on the outer edge and follow it until you have outlined the entire cookie. Use the same piping bag of cerise pink buttercream to fill in the cookie using a zig-zag motion. Repeat this step with all the cookies.

3. When the cookie is filled in completely, use the small offset spatula to smooth out the buttercream (see tips for smoothing buttercream in the Cookie Basics section on page 9). Repeat this step with all the cookies.

(continued)

4. Fill a piping bag fitted with a #1 Wilton piping tip with pine buttercream. Starting on the far-left leaf, make a straight line through the center of the leaf. Place the tip of the buttercream bag perpendicular to the cookie surface, starting at the tip of the far-left leaf. Gently apply pressure as you lift slightly upward, allowing the buttercream to fall to the cookie surface. Slowly release pressure, ending the line near the stem. Add the needles by placing the tip of the buttercream bag parallel to the cookie surface, starting at the top of the line and gently applying pressure as you lift slightly upward, allowing the buttercream to fall to the cookie surface, ending at the outer edge of the leaf. Repeat this step on both halves until the leaf is filled in completely with lines.

5. Fill in the second leaf using the technique in step 4.

6. Fill a piping bag fitted with a #1 Wilton piping tip with mocha buttercream. Starting at the tip of the stem, place the tip of the piping bag perpendicular to the cookie and gently apply pressure as you lift slightly upward, allowing the buttercream to fall to the cookie surface. Slowly release pressure, ending the line near the midpoint of each pinecone. Using the same technique as for the stems, create the outline for each of the pinecones.

7. Replace the #1 piping tip with a #5 Wilton piping tip on the piping bag of mocha buttercream. Fill in the pinecone outlines using a circular motion. Repeat steps 4 through 7 with all the cookies.

8. When both pinecone outlines are filled in completely, use the small offset spatula to smooth out the buttercream.

9. Replace the #5 piping tip with a #81 Wilton piping tip on the piping bag of mocha buttercream. Add additional buttercream to the piping bag as needed. Starting at the tip of the pinecone shape, place the tip of the piping bag against the cookie surface with the concave side of the tip facing downward. Gently apply pressure as you pull downward, releasing pressure once you have created a ¼-inch (6-mm) length of buttercream. Start the second row, repeating the technique and overlapping halfway down the first row. Continue until the entire pinecone is filled in.

10. Repeat step 9 on the second pinecone.

11. Fill a piping bag fitted with a #5 Wilton piping tip with the ruby buttercream. Holding the piping bag at a 90° angle with the tip of the bag against the cookie surface, gently apply pressure, creating dots of varying size for berries.

12. Repeat steps 8 through 11 with the remaining cookies. Refill the piping bags with buttercream as needed. Leftover buttercream can be stored in an airtight container in the fridge for up to 1 week and in the freezer for up to 3 months.

STENCILS

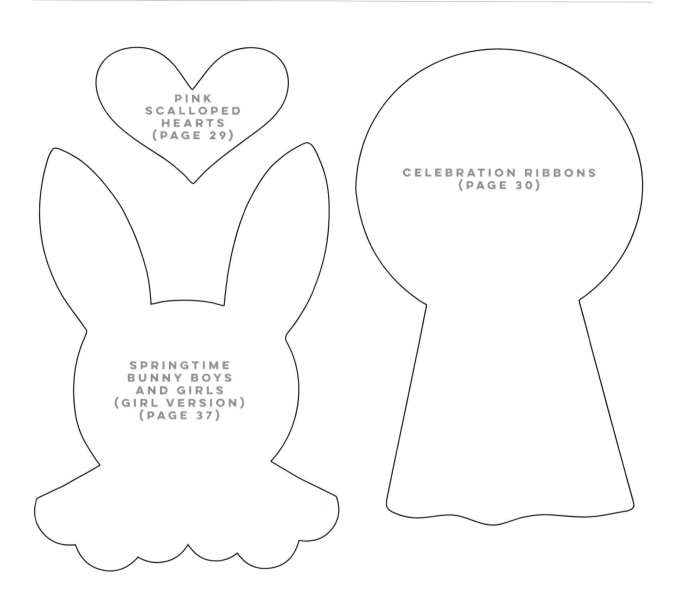

PINK
SCALLOPED
HEARTS
(PAGE 29)

SPRINGTIME
BUNNY BOYS
AND GIRLS
(GIRL VERSION)
(PAGE 37)

CELEBRATION RIBBONS
(PAGE 30)

SPRINGTIME
BUNNY BOYS
AND GIRLS
(BOY VERSION)
(PAGE 37)

DAINTY DAISIES
(PAGE 47)

CHEERY CHICKS
(PAGE 41)

BLOOMING
TULIPS
(PAGE 48)

CHOLLA MINIS
(PAGE 59)

PRICKLY
PEARS
(PAGE 64)

DESERT
LIGHTNING
BUGS
(PAGE 67)

LOVELY LITTLE LLAMAS
(PAGE 55)

GOLDEN WILD
FLOWERS
(PAGE 71)

BUG WINGS
(PAGE 67)

FALL FLORAL
PUMPKINS
(VERSION 3)
(PAGE 77)

FALL FLORAL PUMPKINS
(VERSION 1)(PAGE 77)

FALL FLORAL PUMPKINS
(VERSION 2)(PAGE 77)

RUSTIC
FALL LEAVES
(PAGE 91)

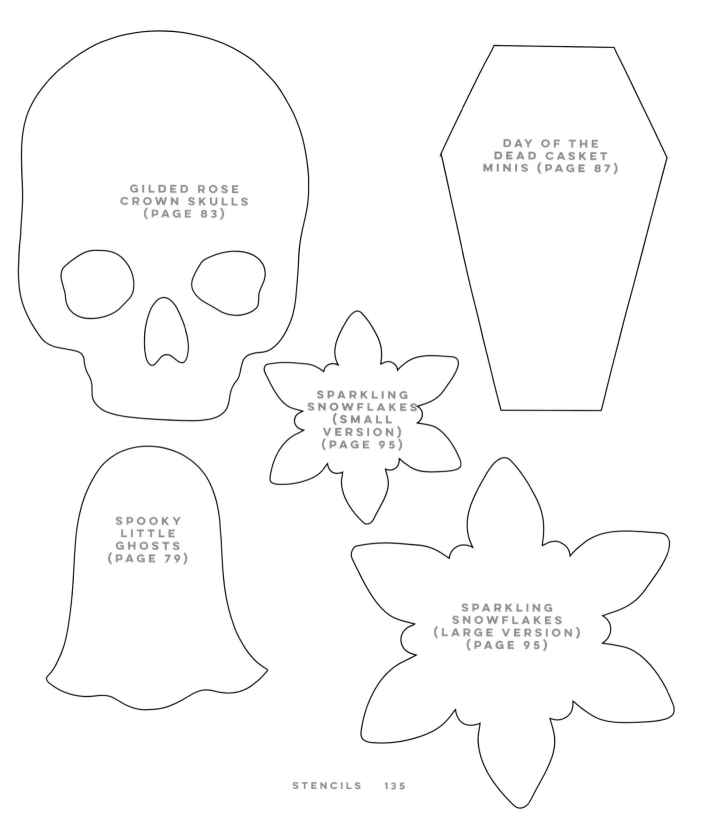

GILDED ROSE
CROWN SKULLS
(PAGE 83)

DAY OF THE
DEAD CASKET
MINIS (PAGE 87)

SPARKLING
SNOWFLAKES
(SMALL
VERSION)
(PAGE 95)

SPOOKY
LITTLE
GHOSTS
(PAGE 79)

SPARKLING
SNOWFLAKES
(LARGE VERSION)
(PAGE 95)

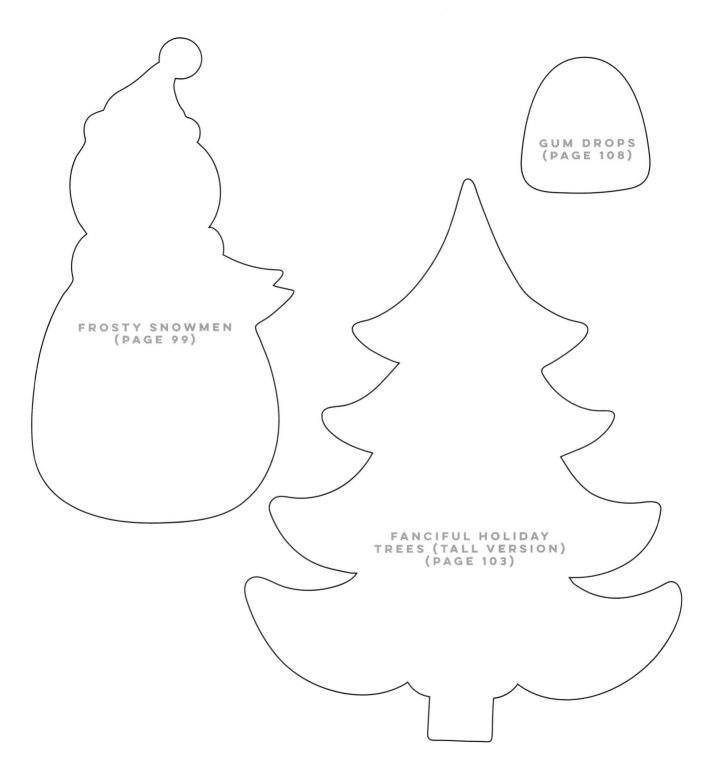

GUM DROPS
(PAGE 108)

FROSTY SNOWMEN
(PAGE 99)

FANCIFUL HOLIDAY
TREES (TALL VERSION)
(PAGE 103)

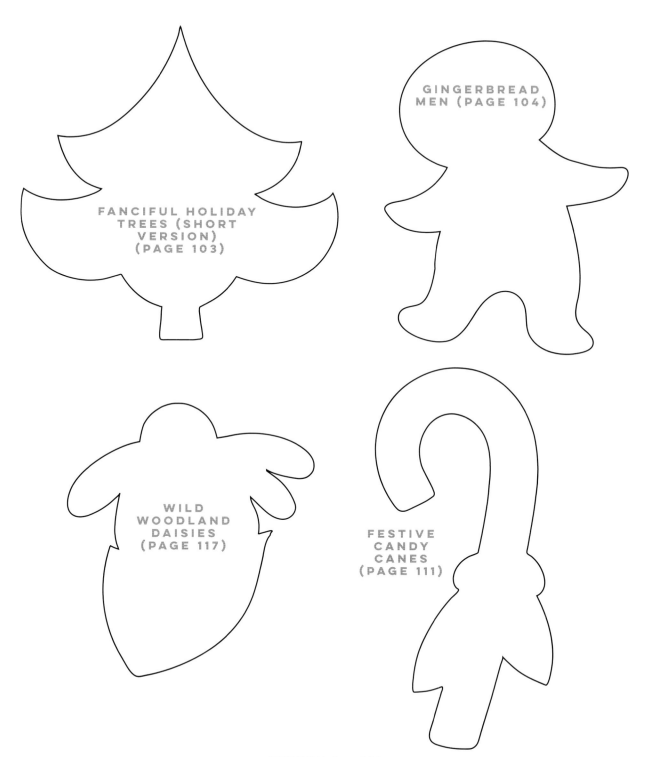

FANCIFUL HOLIDAY
TREES (SHORT
VERSION)
(PAGE 103)

GINGERBREAD
MEN (PAGE 104)

WILD
WOODLAND
DAISIES
(PAGE 117)

FESTIVE
CANDY
CANES
(PAGE 111)

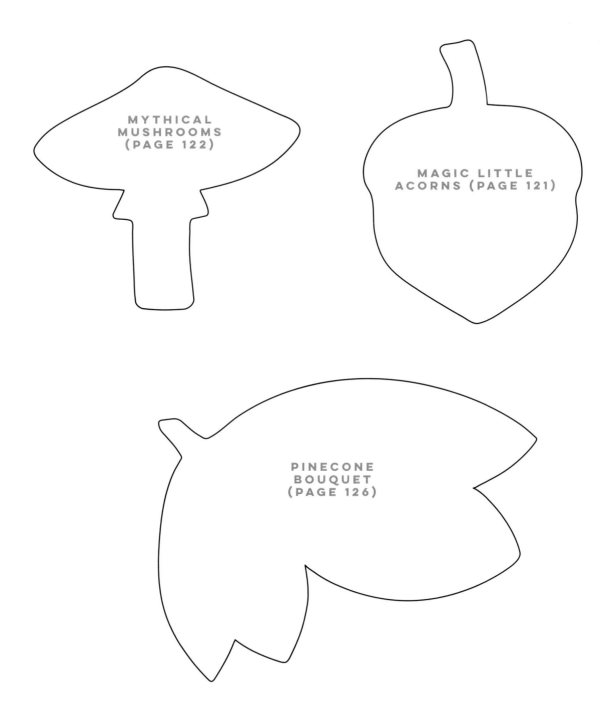

MYTHICAL
MUSHROOMS
(PAGE 122)

MAGIC LITTLE
ACORNS (PAGE 121)

PINECONE
BOUQUET
(PAGE 126)

ACKNOWLEDGMENTS

To my editor Franny Donington, thank you for your patience and for helping me navigate through unfamiliar publishing territory, for all your insight, for believing in the creative process, all while polishing my words and tailoring my ideas into an amazing book.

To Paula Rey, because you have been there always, for everything—for being my biggest cheerleader, for never giving up on me and for all the walks and wisdom. I don't know where I would be without you.

To Debbie, for loving my dad and caring for him in his final days, for continuing to be a powerhouse of strength and kindness. You were there when I needed you most and I will be forever grateful.

To Grandma Helen, thank you for letting me watch you pipe out roses. My six-year-old self thought you were pure magic—I now know how magical you really were.

To Tony, for being an amazing and funny friend and taking care of the fur babies so I could have the occasional break.

To Amajit, for making my days fun, and for reminding me to care for myself first and that food is an act of love.

To Skyba, thank you for all your support and generosity. Your strength and courage as a mother has taught me so much about community and the power a mother has to shape the world. You are amazing.

To Scott, for being an amazing friend and supportive of all my dreams, for recognizing my skills in photography and encouraging me to go further and for all the love you gave to my sweet boy Jasper.

To Meredith, thank you for all the coffee dates and listening to all things Sugarbombe, for all your encouragement and excitement around baking and for always showing up to bake at the church. It was a truly special time, and I'm grateful you were there and continue to be here to bake and create.

To Mom, thank you for always letting me help in the kitchen; you shaped and encouraged my love of food and baking at a very impressionable age. It's the greatest gift to have received.

To Dad, for teaching me to have a voice, but mostly for teaching me that my voice matters. I will love you forever.

To Lilly and Elsa, for letting me live in your wonderous world, for the girl hangs on the trampoline, for letting me hold your hands on Sunday roller skate dates, for all the bedtime stories, for letting me teach you about food, but most of all for showing me how amazing life is through your eyes.

To the readers and supporters of Sugarbombe, thank you for all your endless words of kindness and encouragement. It takes a village and I'm so happy you are all in my village. I wouldn't have this book without each and every one of you.

ABOUT THE AUTHOR

Melissa Broyles is a graduate of Seattle Culinary Academy. She is a lifelong baker, recipe developer, food photographer, designer and the creator of Sugarbombe.

INDEX